McCall's
Needlework

150
Best-Loved
Christmas
Ornaments

McCall's Needlework
150 Best-Loved Christmas Ornaments
from the *Best of McCall's Needlework* series

©1995 by Oxmoor House, Inc.
Book Division of Southern Progress Corporation
P.O. Box 2463
Birmingham, Alabama 35201

Published by Oxmoor House, Inc., Leisure Arts, Inc., and
Symbol of Excellence Publishers, Inc.

Library of Congress
Catalog Card Number: 94-067755
Hardcover ISBN: 0-8487-1436-9
Softcover ISBN: 0-8487-1466-0
Manufactured in the United States of America
First Printing 1995

Oxmoor House, Inc.

Editor-in-Chief: Nancy J. Fitzpatrick
Senior Crafts Editor: Susan Ramey Cleveland
Senior Editor, Editorial Services: Olivia Kindig Wells
Associate Production Manager: Theresa L. Beste
Production Assistant: Marianne Jordan

Symbol of Excellence Publishers, Inc.

Executive Editors: Barbara Cockerham, Phyllis Hoffman
Editor: Diane Kennedy-Jackson
Editorial Assistant: Susan Branch
Production Manager: Wayne Hoffman
Associate Production Manager: Perry James
Creative Director: Mac Jamieson
Executive Art Director: Yukie McLean
Art Director: Michael Whisenant
Graphic Designers: Dottie Barton, Scott Begley, Rick Nance
Photographer: David L. Maxwell
Photography Stylists: Michael Jones, Cathy Muir,
    Jarinda Wiechman

Contents

You are cordially invited to join us in a seasonal celebration of needlework. Turn the page to begin your journey into the magical, wonder-filled world of Christmas!

Shades of White

Elegance comes in many forms, but we know of no more luxurious way to convey it than in the simple beauty of white. Included within the pages of this chapter is a variety of projects that shows the versatility of decorating for the holidays using white, both alone and in combination with delicate, pastel hues or shimmering metallics. From crochet angels, snowflakes, and ornament covers, to gorgeous Battenberg lace, and ecru-on-ecru embroidery, these yuletide treasures are certain to delight you. Use them to adorn your own home or give them away to add a dash of cheer to a special someone's holiday season.

Battenberg Lace Ornaments

Handmade, lace ornaments will be splendid additions to an oh-so-feminine powder room. Use them to adorn a basket filled with hand towels or, if you have a window in your bathroom, suspend them where they'll float in the sunshine, and let your guests enjoy an unexpected decorative touch.

Note: For these projects, a general materials list and instructions have been given. Specific materials and instructions for each project have been listed separately.

General materials:
1 ball white #12 pearl cotton
Light-colored basting thread
Brown paper
#20 embroidery needle
Hand-sewing needle
Dritz® Fray-Check™
Scissors

General instructions:
1. Transfer patterns to brown paper.
2. Pin Battenberg lace tape to paper pattern, pulling heavy gathering thread on either side of tape to fit around curves. For points, make a fold rather than cutting. Baste tape to paper pattern.
Note: Battenberg lace tape is woven of fine threads, with a heavier free thread running inside each edge; these are called "pull threads" and are used to shape tape to pattern. Width of tape may change slightly as it follows the pattern. Match outer edge to pattern lines in order to have adjacent loops touching.
3. Trim ends of lace tape short and apply dots of Fray-Check™ on the raw ends. Tack overlapping tape together with one or two small stitches.
Note: Side facing you is wrong side.
4. Fill in spaces using needleweaving techniques, as indicated in specific instructions for each ornament. To work stitches, thread embroidery needle with one strand pearl cotton. Knot one end; then, with knot on top, weave along edge of tape a few times before beginning to stitch. As you stitch, pass needle back and forth from one edge of tape to the opposite

edge. Keep an even tension; do not pull thread tightly. End thread by weaving back and forth through tape.
5. After ornaments are assembled, remove basting threads. Rinse piece in cool water and dry flat.
6. Attach bow and/or hanging loop.

Butterfly
Materials:
40" length 5mm Battenberg lace tape
7" length ⅛"-wide burgundy satin ribbon (for hanger)

1. Work Sorrento wheel with three or four twirls in eye of wings.
2. Work gathered straight stitch for top area of wings and tails, gathering four threads at each end and five threads in the middle sections.
3. Work Russian stitch for body and bottom area of wings.

Water Lily
Materials:
30" length 5mm Battenberg lace tape
7" length ⅛"-wide burgundy satin ribbon (for hanger)

1. Work net stitch in uppermost left and right petals.
2. Work Sorrento wheel in remaining petals and center, working four or five twirls in center.
3. Fill small areas with weaving stitch in the shape of an X.

Star
Materials:
36" length 5mm Battenberg lace tape
7" length ⅛"-wide burgundy satin ribbon (for hanger)

1. Work straight stitches in star, forming a base for weaving; then work weaving stitches. Work one or two twirls between each cross thread.

2. Work Sorrento wheel with two twirls in star's points.

Heart
Materials:
20" length 8mm Battenberg lace tape
18" length ⅛"-wide burgundy satin ribbon (for hanger and hanging loop)

1. Work Sorrento wheel with five twirls in center of small heart.
2. Work weaving stitch with wheels, with one twirl between each cross thread between outer and inner hearts.
3. Work picot around outside of heart.

Luna Moth
Materials:
42" length 5mm Battenberg lace tape
7" length ⅛"-wide burgundy satin ribbon (for hanger)

1. Work Sorrento wheel with two twirls in eyes of wings.
2. Work gathering straight stitch around eyes of wings, gathering four threads at each end and five threads in the middle sections.
3. Work Russian stitch for body, tail sections, and bottom wing loops.

Double Ball
Materials:
18" length 8mm Battenberg lace tape
18" length ⅛"-wide burgundy satin ribbon (for hanger and hanging loop)

1. Work Sorrento wheel with five or six twirls in center of small ball.
2. Work Russian stitch between outer and inner balls.
3. Work picot around outside of ball.

NET STITCH

RUSSIAN STITCH

LUNA
MOTH

HEART

STAR

DOUBLE BALL

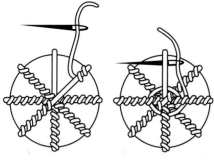

SORRENTO WHEEL

Work one long stitch end to end; then wrap thread back to the center. Work another long stitch to the side and wrap back. Continue until all spokes are made. (**Note:** The first half of the first spoke will not be wrapped yet.) Weave thread over and under long stitches in center of wheel to form hub. When number of twirls indicated in individual instructions is complete, wrap along first half of first spoke to tape.

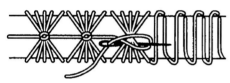

GATHERING STRAIGHT STITCH

Loosely work straight stitches as marked. Gather number of threads, as indicated in individual instructions, beginning at center of area.

WEAVING STITCH WITH WHEELS

Work straight stitches all the way around area; then wrap stitches. End thread. Repeat with cross-over stitches under first group. On the return, work two or three weaving stitches to center each crossover; then work two twirls and wrap remainder of straight stitch.

BUTTERFLY

WATER LILY

WEAVING STITCH

Christmas Snowflakes

This set of six dazzling tree trimmers will provide a wonder-ful opportunity to work with metallic fibers. Stitched with metallic braid and blending filament and completed with an assortment of decorative beads, these delightful pieces will be breathtaking additions to a holiday evergreen.

Note: For these projects, a general materials list has been given. Specific materials and instructions for each project have been listed separately.

General materials:
One 5" square 22-count white Hardanger from Zweigart® (for **each** ornament)
One 11mm clear teardrop crystal prism (for **each** ornament)
White sewing thread (for attaching beads and prisms and for assembling ornaments)
Hand-sewing needle
Tapestry needle
Polyester filling
Measuring tape
Scissors

Note: Please read instructions carefully before beginning. Each square on the chart represents one thread of fabric.

Instructions: Work stitches using one strand #8 braid or two strands blending filament. Attach beads using white sewing thread after stitching is complete.

Red & Gold Snowflake

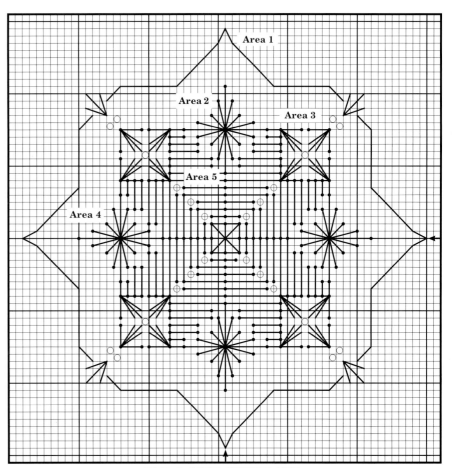

RED & GOLD SNOWFLAKE

Kreinik Metallics	Color
002	gold, #8 braid
003	red, blending filament

Mill Hill Seed Beads	
○ 557	gold

Stitch count: 58H x 58W

Design size:

14-count	4⅛" x 4⅛"
18-count	3¼" x 3¼"
22-count	2⅝" x 2⅝"
25-count	2⅜" x 2⅜"

Area 1: Backstitch over two squares, using two strands 003.
Area 2: Work straight stitch using two strands 003, working from the outer edge into the center hole.
Area 3: Work straight stitch using two strands 003.
Area 4: Work eyelet stitch in center of design, using two strands 003.
Area 5: Work satin stitch using one strand 002.

Green & Silver Snowflake

Kreinik Metallics Color

001	silver, #8 braid
008	green, blending filament

Mill Hill Seed Beads

○ 2010   ice

Eagle Craft Beads

◇ 2mm   silver
■ 3mm   silver

Stitch count: 64H x 64W
Design size:

14-count	4½" x 4½"
18-count	3½" x 3½"
22-count	2⅞" x 2⅞"
25-count	2½" x 2½"

Area 1: Backstitch over two squares, using two strands 008.
Area 2: Work straight stitch using two strands 008.
Area 3: Work Algerian eye stitch using two strands 008.
Area 4: Work satin stitch using one strand 001.

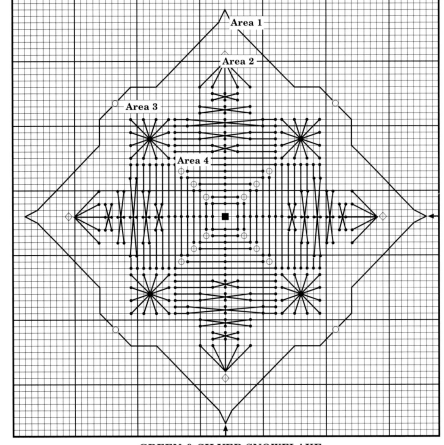

GREEN & SILVER SNOWFLAKE

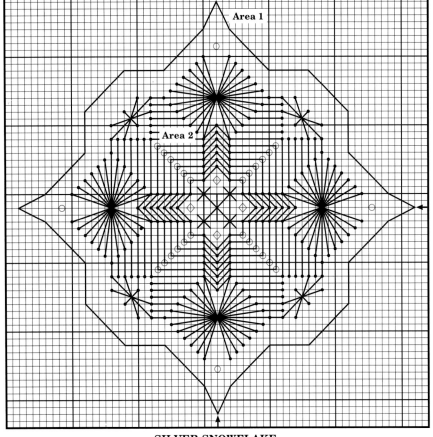

SILVER SNOWFLAKE

Silver Snowflake

Kreinik Metallics Color

101	platinum, #8 braid
041	confetti pink, blending filament

Mill Hill Seed Beads

○ 2010   ice

Eagle Craft Beads

◇ 2mm   silver

Stitch count: 60H x 60W
Design size:

14-count	4¼" x 4¼"
18-count	3⅜" x 3⅜"
22-count	2¾" x 2¾"
25-count	2⅜" x 2⅜"

Area 1: Backstitch over two squares, using two strands 041.
Area 2: Work satin stitch using one strand 101.
Work remainder of design in straight stitch, using two strands 041.

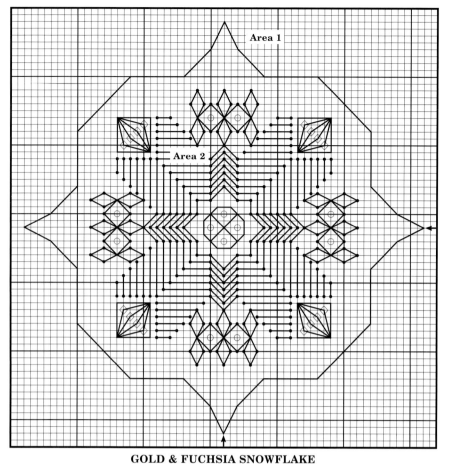

GOLD & FUCHSIA SNOWFLAKE

Gold & Fuchsia Snowflake

Kreinik

Metallics	Color
102	Vatican gold, #8 braid
042	confetti fuchsia, blending filament

Mill Hill Seed Beads

◇	557	gold
○	161	crystal

Stitch count: 60H x 60W

Design size:

14-count	4¼" x 4¼"
18-count	3⅜" x 3⅜"
22-count	2¾" x 2¾"
25-count	2⅜" x 2⅜"

Area 1: Backstitch over two squares, using two strands 042.

Area 2: Work satin stitch using one strand 102.

Work remainder of design in straight stitch, using two strands 042.

Silver & Blue Snowflake

Kreinik

Metallics	Color
001	silver, #8 braid
044	confetti blue, blending filament

Mill Hill Seed Beads

○	2010	ice

Eagle Craft Beads

◇	2mm	silver
■	3mm	silver

Stitch count: 62H x 62W

Design size:

14-count	4½" x 4½"
18-count	3½" x 3½"
22-count	2⅞" x 2⅞"
25-count	2½" x 2½"

Area 1: Backstitch over two squares, using two strands 044.

Area 2: Work diamond eyelet stitch using two strands 044.

Area 3: Work straight stitch using two strands 044.

Area 4: Work satin stitch using one strand 001.

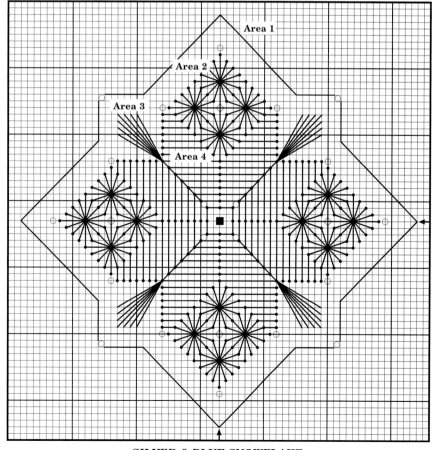

SILVER & BLUE SNOWFLAKE

Gold Snowflake

Kreinik Metallics	Color
002	gold, #8 braid
043	confetti green, blending filament

Mill Hill Seed Beads

○ 557	gold
● 161	crystal

Stitch count: 60H x 60W
Design size:

14-count	4¼" x 4¼"
18-count	3⅜" x 3⅜"
22-count	2¾" x 2¾"
25-count	2⅜" x 2⅜"

Area 1: Backstitch over two squares, using two strands 043.
Area 2: Work diamond eyelet stitch using two strands 043.
Area 3: Work straight stitch using two strands 043.
Area 4: Work Smyrna cross stitch in center of design, using two strands 043.
Area 5: Work satin stitch using one strand 002.

Finishing instructions:
1. Complete stitching following instructions given.
2. Make a twisted-cord hanging loop using a 36" length of Fine (#8) Braid in color used for ornament, referring

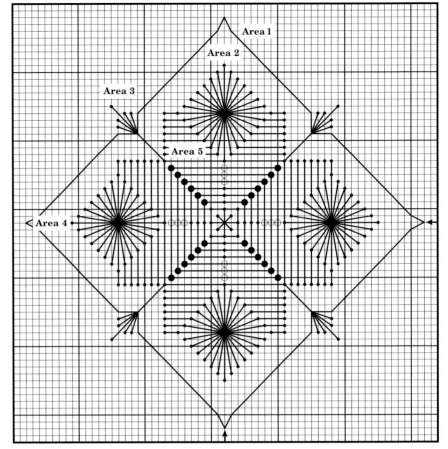

GOLD SNOWFLAKE

to "How-Tos for Making Twisted Cording" on page **141**. Set aside.
3. Referring to Finishing Illustration, count up fifteen threads from backstitched border and trim away excess fabric. Turn edges under five threads and baste in place. Bring

Point A together with Point B, turning edges of fabric to inside of ornament. Tack and, following arrows, sew fabric edges together up to the point. Attach hanging loop before closing off the end. Bring needle back down to Point B from the inside. Bring Point C together with Point B, turning edge of fabric to inside of ornament. Tack and, following arrows, sew fabric edges together out to the point. Return to Point C from the inside. Bring Point D together with Point C, tack and, following arrows, sew fabric edges together down to the point. Tack crystal prism at this point (opposite hanger). Return to Point D. Stuff ornament firmly with polyester filling. Sew the last seam, following arrows, to complete ornament.

FINISHING ILLUSTRATION

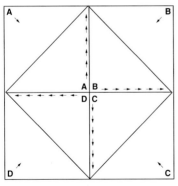

EYELET STITCH

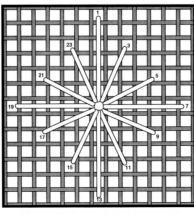

SATIN STITCH

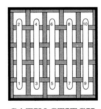

DIAMOND EYELET STITCH

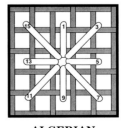

ALGERIAN EYE STITCH

SMYRNA CROSS STITCH

16

Tatted Snowflakes

Tiny, tatted, sparkling snowflakes will look wonderful hanging from the branches of an evergreen, and they can also serve a dual purpose when used as festive favors. Make your next holiday dinner party an unforgettable treat by sending each of your guests home with a shimmering ornament. It's certain to remind them of a special evening in your home each time they place it on their Christmas tree.

Tatting abbreviations:
ch(s)—chain(s)
cl—close
ds—double stitch
j—join
lg—large-sized
p(s)—picot(s)
r(s)—ring(s)
reg—regular-sized
rw—reverse work
sep—separated

Materials:
One 5-m. reel Kreinik 1/16" ribbon, #102
   Vatican gold **or** #001 silver
Tatting shuttle
Scissors

Finished size: 2" diameter

Wind ribbon on shuttle, leaving reel attached.
r: 1ds, reg p, 1ds, lg p, rep working 1ds and alternating reg p and lg p until 4 reg ps and 3 lg ps, end with 1ds, cl, rw.
ch: 2ds, 3p sep by 2ds, 2ds, rw.
Work second and all other rs same as first.
Second, third, and fourth chs of 2ds, join to last p of last ch, 2ds, 2ps sep by 2ds, 2ds, rw.
Alternate rs and second chs until 5 rs and 4 chs.
Last ch of 2ds, join to last p of last ch, 2ds, p, 2ds, join to first p of first ch, 2ds. Cut threads 6" long and tie to base of first r. Tie ends of threads together to form hanger.

Opals in the Snow

The fire and brilliance of opals are captured in this beaded, needlepoint ornament. Beautiful shading gives lavender and rose floss an opalescent look. Try hanging the Opals in the Snow *ornament on a crystal decanter this Christmas season, and enjoy the sparkle of metallic floss and beads in reflected light.*

	DMC	Color
C	225	pink, vy. lt.
⌐	3042	antique violet, lt.
/	3721	pink, dk.
	791	cornflower, vy. dk.

Needle Necessities overdyed floss

○	160	festiva
□	175	Bavarian grape
X	176	heather on the hill
♥	191	harlequin

Kreinik medium (#16) braid

◆	012	purple
•	093	star mauve
✳	209HL	heather hi-luster

Kreinik ⅛" ribbon

042	confetti fuchsia
095	starburst

AK Designs beads

⊃	418	grape 11/0
+	302C	blossom pink 8/0

Fabric: 18-count Lavendula mono canvas from Access Commodities (**Note:** Cut mono canvas 10" square.)
Stitch count: 66H x 66W
Design size:

14-count	4¾" x 4¾"
16-count	4⅛" x 4⅛"
18-count	3⅝" x 3⅝"
22-count	3" x 3"

Instructions: Work design using tent stitch in basketweave pattern, using six strands of floss. Work running stitches using Kreinik ⅛" ribbon. Work weaving using six strands overdyed floss. Work stitches using #24 tapestry needle. Attach beads using two strands 160 and #10 beading needle.

Running-stitch instructions:

095	center square, middle border, top and right side of outer border
042	bottom and left side of outer border

Weaving instructions:

175	top and right side of outer border
191	bottom and left side of outer border, center square
791	middle border

Finishing instructions:
Materials:
Two 8" squares lavender fabric (for lining and backing)
¾ yd. ¼"-diameter purple purchased twisted cording
1 yd. ⅛"-diameter coral purchased twisted cording
One 5-m. reel 9300 orchid Kreinik 1/16" ribbon
1 yd. 1"-wide purple sheer ribbon
Polyester filling
Hand-sewing needle
Scissors
Sewing machine

1. Complete stitching following instructions given.
2. Trim canvas to within 1" of edge of stitching. Trim lavender fabric squares to same size as canvas. Baste canvas to fabric ½" from stitching to line front. Sew stitched front to back, placing right sides of fabric together and sewing two canvas threads from edge of stitching. Leave top-left and bottom-right corners open. These will be top and bottom points of ornament. Trim seams and clip corners. Turn right-side out.
3. Make a tassel using heather on the hill overdyed floss and orchid 1/16"

ribbon, referring to tassel-making instructions on page **101** and wrapping floss and ribbon around a 4" card.
4. Form a hanger using 8"-length coral twisted cord. Insert cord ends in top opening and tack in place. Whipstitch opening closed.
5. Beginning at bottom point, tack coral twisted cord along seam line. Tack purple twisted cord behind coral.
6. Make a four-loop bow from 1" ribbon. Sew around center of bow with ribbon tie of tassel.
7. Stuff ornament with polyester filling. Turn ends of cording to inside. Tack tassel and bow to bottom point. Whipstitch opening closed.

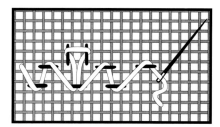

SIDE WEAVING

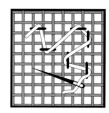

CORNER WEAVING

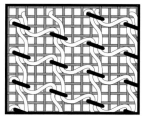

CENTER WEAVING

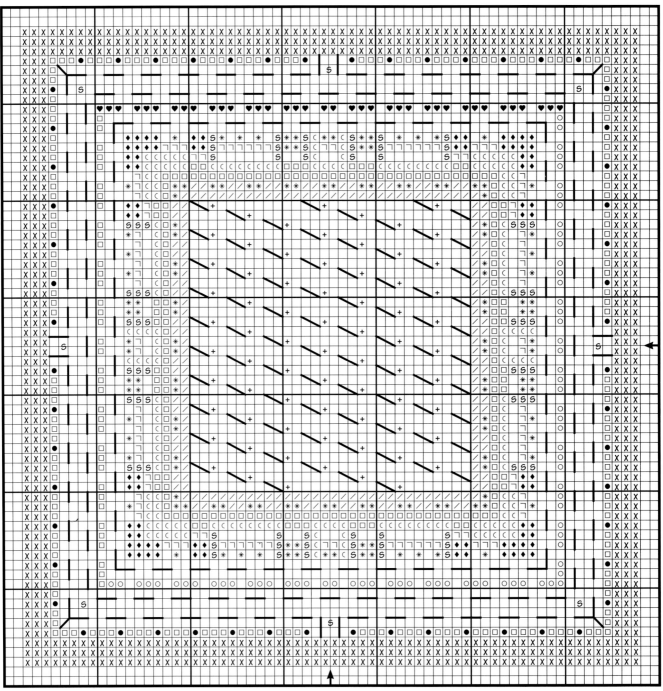

OPALS IN THE SNOW

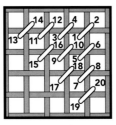

**TENT STITCH
BASKETWEAVE
METHOD**

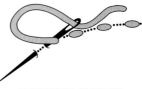

RUNNING STITCH

Crochet Ornament Covers

White crochet covers form gorgeous trims, transforming plain glass-ball ornaments into treasured holiday heirlooms. The ribbon and bead colors can be changed to complement any color glass ball, making these designs so versatile that they can be used with almost any color decorating theme.

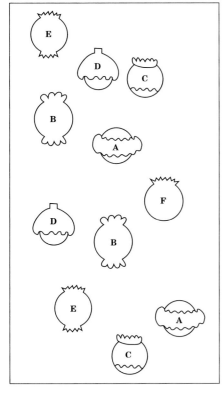

Crochet Ornament Covers

Crochet Abbreviations:
bet—between
ch—chain stitch
cont—continue
dc—double crochet
est—established
lp(s)—loop(s)
nxt—next
rep—repeat
rnd(s)—round(s)
sc—single crochet
sk—skip
sl—slip
sl st—slip stitch
sp(s)—space(s)
st—stitch
tog—together
tr—treble
WS—wrong side(s)
yo—yarn over

Note: For these projects, a general materials list has been given. Specific materials and instructions for each project have been listed separately. Each ornament cover measures approximately 3" in diameter.

General materials:
One 350-yd. ball white Coats & Clark Big Ball crochet cotton, Art. B.34 size #30 (makes four ornaments)
3" red **or** silver Christmas ball ornament (for **each** ornament cover)
⅛"-wide red and white satin ribbon
Steel #12 (.6mm) crochet hook

Lacy Wrap **(A)**
Materials:
½ yd. ⅛"-wide red satin ribbon (for **each** *Lacy Wrap*)

Ch 107.
Rnd 1: Dc in 8th ch from hook, * ch 2, sk 2, dc in nxt ch; rep from * across. Do not turn.
Rnd 2: Ch 2 (counts as 1 sc), 2 sc in same st (corner made), 2 sc in end sp, 3 sc in nxt corner st; * 2 sc in sp, sc in dc; rep from * across. Working 3 sc in corners, cont along opposite side as est. Join with sl st in starting ch-2. Sl st to 2nd sc of corner 3-sc.
Rnd 3: Ch 6 (counts as dc and ch 3), dc in same st, ch 3, sk 3 sc, (dc, ch 3, dc) in 2nd sc of corner 3-sc, ch 3, sk 3, (dc,

ch 3, dc) in nxt sc; * ch 3, sk 2, (dc, ch 3, dc) in nxt sc; rep from * across, working ch 3, sk 3, (dc, ch 3, dc) in 2nd st of corner 3-sc. Cont as est along opposite side. Join with sl st in 3rd ch of starting ch-6.
Rnd 4: Sl st in ch-3 sp (corner), ch 6 (counts as dc and ch 3), dc in same sp, * ch 3, (dc, ch 3, dc) in nxt sp; rep from * around. Join with sl st in 3rd ch of starting ch-6. Sl st in ch-3 sp (corner).
Rnd 5: Ch 6 (counts as dc and ch 3), sl st in 3rd ch from hook (picot made), dc in same ch-3 sp; holding back last lp on both, 2 dc in nxt sp, yo and through 3 lps on hook (2-dc cluster made), ch 3, cluster in same sp; * (dc, picot, dc) in nxt sp, (cluster, ch 3, cluster) in nxt sp; rep from * around. Join with sl st in 3rd ch of starting ch-6. End off.
Finishing:
Thread ribbon through mesh in center of lace. Wrap crocheted lace around ornament and tie with bow at top.

Candy Wrapper **(B)**
Materials:
1 yd. ⅛"-wide white satin ribbon (for **each** *Candy Wrapper*)
162 3mm white pearl beads (for **each** *Candy Wrapper*)
Beading needle

Thread all beads onto crochet cotton.
Rnd 1: Ch 115, draw up bead, sk 8 ch, sl st in nxt ch (with bead in front of work); ch 3, sk 2, dc in nxt ch; ch 5, sk 5, dc in nxt ch; * ch 3, sk 2, draw up bead, sl st in nxt ch (securing bead); ch 3, sk 2, dc in nxt ch; ch 5, sk 5, dc in nxt ch; rep from * across. Join with sl st in 4th ch from starting bead.
Rnd 2: Ch 8 (counts as dc and ch 5), dc in nxt dc, ch 3, sk 3, draw up bead (holding in front of work), sl st in nxt ch (securing bead); ch 3, sk 2, dc in nxt dc; * ch 5, sk 5, dc in nxt dc; ch 3, sk 2, draw up bead, sl st in nxt dc; ch 3, sk 2, dc in ch; rep from * around. Join with sl st in 3rd ch of starting ch-8.
Rnd 3: Ch 6 (counts as dc and ch 3), sk 2, draw up bead, sl st in nxt ch; ch 3, sk 2, dc in nxt dc; ch 5, sk 5, dc in nxt dc; * ch 3, sk 2, draw up bead, sl st in nxt ch; ch 3, sk 2, dc in dc; ch 5, sk 5, dc in nxt dc; rep from * around. Join with sl st in 3rd ch of starting ch-6.
Rnds 4–18: Rep Rnds 2 and 3, ending after Rnd 2.
Top Edge—Rnd 1: Ch 5 (counts as dc and ch 2), sk 2, dc in nxt ch; ch 2,

sk 2, dc in nxt dc; ch 5, dc in nxt dc; * (ch 2, sk 2, dc in nxt st) twice; ch 5, dc in nxt dc; rep from * around. Join with sl st in 3rd ch of starting ch-5.
Rnd 2 (eyelet rnd): Ch 5 (counts as dc and ch 2), sk 2, dc in nxt st; * ch 2, sk 2, dc in nxt st; rep from * around. Join with sl st in 3rd ch of starting ch-5.
Rnd 3: Ch 1, sc in joining, * 2 sc in sp, 1 sc in dc; rep from * around. Join with sl st in starting sc.
Rnd 4: Ch 6 (counts as dc and ch 3), dc in joining; * ch 3, sk 2, (dc, ch 3, dc) in nxt st; rep from * around. Join with sl st in 3rd ch of starting ch-6.
Rnd 5: Ch 6 (counts as dc and ch 3), sl st in 3rd ch from hook (picot made), dc in same sp; holding back last lp on both, 2 dc in nxt sp, yo and through 3 lps on hook (2-dc cluster made), ch 3, cluster in same sp; * (dc, picot, dc) in nxt sp, (cluster, ch 3, cluster) in nxt sp; rep from * around. Join with sl st in 3rd ch of starting ch-6. End off.
Lower Edge—Rnds 1–4: Work as for top edge, starting with Rnd 2.
Finishing:
Cut ribbon in half. Thread each piece through eyelet rnds of upper and lower edges. Insert ornament and draw cover closed. Tie ribbons in bows.

Beaded Fancy Half-Wrap **(C)**
Materials:
½ yd. ⅛"-wide white satin ribbon (for **each** *Beaded Fancy Half-Wrap*)
81 3mm white pearl beads (for **each** *Beaded Fancy Half-Wrap*)
Beading needle

Thread beads onto crochet cotton.
Rnds 1–3: Rep Rnds 1–3 of *Candy Wrapper*.
Rnds 4–9: Rep Rnds 2 and 3 alternately.
Top Edge—Rnd 1: Ch 8 (counts as dc and ch 5), dc in dc; * (ch 2, sk 2, dc in nxt st) twice; ch 5, dc in nxt dc; rep from * around. Join with sl st in 3rd ch of starting ch-8.
Rnds 2–5 (eyelet rnd): Rep Top Edge Rnds 2–5 of *Candy Wrapper*. End off.
Lower Edge: Attach thread in ch-5 sp, ch 1; * (3 sc, ch 5, 3 sc) in each sp around. Join with sl st in first sc. End off.
Finishing:
Thread ribbon through Rnd 2 of Top Edge. Insert ornament and draw closed. Tie ribbon in a bow.

Floral Half-Wrap (D)

Ch 6, sl st in 6th ch from hook to form a ring. Work from bottom to top of ornament.

Rnd 1: * Ch 4 (counts as tr); holding last lp from each on hook, 2 tr in ring, yo and through all 3 lps (3-tr cluster made); ch 4, sl st in top of cluster; ch 4 (counts as tr), sl st in ring *; rep bet *s 3 more times; [Ch 6, sl st in 3rd ch from hook (picot made), ch 9, sl st in 6th ch from hook to form ring; rep bet *s] 11 times. End with ch 6, sl st in 3rd ch from hook, ch 3. Join with sl st in first ring (bet side clusters), ch 1.

Rnd 2: Sl st in ch-3 sp, * ch 6, sl st in 3rd ch from hook (picot made), ch 3, sl st in nxt ch-3 sp; rep from * around (working behind clusters to the nxt sp). Join with sl st in starting sl st.

Rnd 3: Sl st in ch-3 sp, * ch 6, sl st in 3rd ch from hook (picot made), ch 4, picot, ch 3, (draw up lp in nxt ch-3 sp) twice, pulling last lp through all lps on hook; rep from * around. Join by drawing up lp in nxt ch-3 sp and starting sl st, pull last lp through all lps on hook.

Rnds 4–7: Sl st in ch-1 sp, * ch 6, picot, ch 3, sl st in ch-1 sp; rep from * around. Join with sl st in starting sl st.

Rnd 8: Sl st in ch-1 sp, ch 4 (counts as dc and ch 1), * dc in nxt ch-1 sp, ch 1; rep from * around. Join with sl st in 3rd ch of starting ch-4.

Rnd 9: Sl st in ch-1 sp, ch 4 (counts as tr), holding last lp on hook, tr in nxt 2 ch-1 sps, yo and through all lps on hook (3-tr cluster made), ch 1, * 3-tr cluster in nxt 3 sps, ch 1, rep from * around. Join with sl st in top of starting cluster.

Rnd 10: Sl st in sp bet clusters, ch 6 (counts as dc and ch 3), dc, ch 3, dc in sp, * (dc, ch 3) 3 times, dc in nxt sp bet cluster; rep from * around. Join with sl st in 3rd ch of starting ch-6. End off.

Finishing:
Place half-wrap over ornament.

Hairpin-Lace Wrap (E)
Materials:
½ yd. ⅛"-wide red satin ribbon (for **each** *Hairpin-Lace Wrap*)
60 red rocaille beads (for **each** *Hairpin-Lace Wrap*)
1" hairpin-lace pin
Beading needle

Hairpin-Lace Strip (make two):
String 30 beads onto crochet cotton.

Using 1" lace pin, * work 6 lps of hairpin lace, with WS facing, draw up bead, secure to front of work with ch; rep from * until 8" or 93 lps (on each side) and 30 beads have been made. End off. Braid strips together 3 lps at a time.

Lower edge—Rnd 1: * Work 3 sc in each group of 3 hairpin lps held tog; rep from * around. Join with sl st in first sc.

Rnd 2: Ch 3 (counts as dc); holding last lp of each on hook, dc in nxt 2 sc, yo and through all lps (3-dc cluster made), ch 3; * 3-dc cluster in nxt 3 sc, ch 3; rep from * around. Join with sl st in top of starting cluster.

Rnd 3: Sl st in ch-3 sp, ch 3 (counts as dc); holding last lp for each on hook, 2 dc in sp, yo and through all lps (3-dc cluster), ch 1; * 3-dc cluster in nxt sp, ch 1, rep from * around. Join with sl st in top of starting cluster.

Rnd 4: Sl st in sp bet clusters, ch 4 (counts as dc and ch); * dc in nxt sp bet clusters, ch 1; rep from * around. Join with sl st in 3rd ch of starting ch-4.

Rnd 5: Sl st in ch-1 sp, ch 4 (counts as tr); holding last lp on hook, tr in nxt 2 ch-1 sps, yo and through all lps on hook (3-tr cluster made), ch 1; * 3-tr cluster in nxt 3 sps, ch 1; rep from * around. Join with sl st in top of starting cluster.

Rnd 6: Sl st in sp bet clusters, ch 6 (counts as dc and ch 3); dc, ch 3, dc in sp, * (dc, ch 3) 3 times, dc in nxt sp bet clusters; rep from * around. Join with sl st in 3rd ch of starting ch-6. End off.

Top Edge—Rnd 1: * Work 3 sc in each group of 3 hairpin lps held tog; rep from * around. Join with sl st in first sc.

Rnd 2: Ch 4 (counts as tr); holding last lp of each on hook, tr in nxt 2 sc, yo and through all lps (3-tr cluster made), ch 3; * 3-tr cluster in nxt 3 sc; rep from * around. Join with sl st in top of starting cluster.

Rnd 3: Ch 6 (counts as dc and 3 ch); * dc in nxt ch-3 sp bet cluster, ch 3; rep from * around; sl st to 3rd ch of beg ch-6.

Rnd 4: Sl st in ch-3 sp, ch 6 (counts as dc and ch 3); (dc, ch 3, dc, ch 3, dc) in same sp, * (dc, ch 3) 3 times, dc in nxt sp; rep from * around. Join with sl st in 3rd ch of starting ch-6.

Finishing:
Thread ribbon through Rnd 3 of Top Edge. Insert ornament and tie closed with bow.

Broomstick-Lace Wrap (F)
Materials:
¾ yd. ⅛"-wide white satin ribbon (for **each** *Broomstick-Lace Wrap*)
#11 (8mm) knitting needle

Broomstick Lace—Row 1: Ch 109. Sc in 2nd ch from hook and in each ch across.

Row 2: Holding knitting needle in left hand and working from left to right, pull up a lp in each st across (working in back of st), placing lps on needle—109 lps. Do not turn.

Row 3: * Insert hook from right to left through first 3 lps on needle, sl these lps off needle; holding tog as 1 lp, work 3 sc in lp, rep from * across. Do not turn.

Row 4: Rep row 2.

Row 5: * Insert hook from right to left through first 3 lps on needle, sl these lps off needle; holding tog as 1 lp, work sc, ch 5, sl st in 5th ch from hook (picot made), sc in lp; rep from * across. Join with sl st in starting ch.

Top Edge—Rnd 1: Sl st to picot, sl st in picot; * ch 3, sl st in nxt picot; rep from * around. Join with sl st in starting sl st.

Rnd 2: * Sl st, ch 5, sl st in ch-3 sp; rep from * around. Join with sl st in starting sl st.

Rnds 3 & 4: * Sl st, ch 7, sl st in ch-5 sp; rep from * around. Join with sl st in starting sl st.

Rnd 5: Sl st, ch 1, 2 sc, ch 5, sl st in 5th ch from hook (picot made), 2 sc in ch-7 sp; * 2 sc, picot, 2 sc in nxt ch-7 sp; rep from * around. Join with sl st in starting sc. End off.

Lower Edge—Rnd 1: Attach crochet cotton, * sc in 3 sts, ch 7, sl st in 7th ch from hook (picot made); rep from * around. Join with sl st in starting sc. End off.

Finishing:
Cut thirty-five 12"-long strands of crochet cotton. * Fold one strand in half, thread fold through lower picot from back to front, pull ends through loop; rep from * across in each lower picot. Insert ornament. Gather strands at base and tie with separate piece of crochet cotton. Trim to 1½". Tie 10" length of ribbon around base. Thread 15" length of ribbon through Rnd 3 of Top Edge and tie closed with bow.

Petite Guardian Angels

This host of heavenly angels will herald the holiday season in style! Worked from a single pattern, these celestial messengers provide a perfect example of how adding an assortment of accessory pieces to a design can change its look completely. When stiffened, these demure creatures stand by themselves, allowing you limitless decorating possibilities.

Crochet Abbreviations:
beg—beginning
bet—between
ch—chain stitch
dc—double crochet
lp(s)—loop(s)
nxt—next
rnd(s)—round(s)
sc—single crochet
sk—skip
sl st—slip stitch
sp(s)—space(s)
tr—treble
yo—yarn over
(–)—repeat directions number of times given

Terms:
Ch 3 at beginning of row counts as dc.
"V" sp—dc, ch 1, dc in same sp.
To decrease—Insert hook in st, yo, pull lp through st [= 2 lps on hook]; insert hook in nxt st, yo, pull lp through st [= 3 lps on hook]; yo, pull through all 3 lps on hook [= 1 lp on hook].

Materials:
40 yds. DMC Baroque Crochet Cotton Thread, white, Art. 158, size 10 (for **each** ornament)
#8 Boye steel crochet hook
3 small cotton balls (for **each** ornament)
Index card
Stiffening board (i.e. corrugated cardboard **or** meat tray)
Plastic wrap
Tape
Fabric stiffener
Rustproof pins
7" length clear nylon monofilament for **each** ornament (for hanger)
Ribbons, pearls, beads, blossoms, etc. (optional)

Size: Approximately 4"

Head
[Leave 3" tail to use as marker.] Ch 5, sl st in 1st ch to form ring.
Rnd A: Ch 3, 11 dc in ring [12 dc]. **Do not** join rows. Mark rows by weaving beg tail up bet last st on row and 1st st of nxt row through row K.
Rnd B: Make 2 sc in 3rd ch and in each dc—24 sc.
Rnds C–G: Sc in each sc. [Count **as** you work.]
Rnd H: (Sc in nxt sc, decrease nxt sc) rnd—16 sc.
Rnd I: [Insert cotton ball.] Decrease in each sc—8 sc.
Rnd J: Sc in each sc—8 sc.
Rnd K: (Sc in nxt sc, 2 sc in nxt sc) rnd—12 sc. Trim tail.

Bodice
Row 1: Ch 4, (dc in nxt sc, ch 1) 11 times, sl st in 3rd ch and sp at beg of row—12 sps.
Row 2: Ch 5, dc in nxt sp. (Ch 2, dc in nxt sp) 11 times, ch 2, sl st in 3rd ch and sp.

Row 3: Ch 3, 3 dc in same sp. (4 dc in nxt sp) around, sl st in 3rd ch—48 dc.
Row 4: Ch 5, sk 1 dc, (dc nxt dc, ch 2, sk 1 dc) around, sl st in 3rd ch and sp—24 sp. [Use blunt end of hook to complete filling head and neck with cotton balls.]
Row 5: Ch 3, 3 dc in same sp, ch 2 [hole in back for wings later] sk 1 sp, (4 dc in nxt sp, ch 1; sc in nxt sp, ch 1) around, sl st in 3rd ch and nxt dc—12 scallops.

Skirt
Row 6: Sc in nxt dc, ch 3, sk dc, sp and 1 dc, sc in nxt dc, ch 3, sc in nxt dc, ch 1; fold bodice with right side out, sk 4 scallops and 1 dc in 5th scallop, sc in nxt dc, ch 3, sc in nxt dc, ch 3, sk dc, two ch-1 sp and 1 dc, sc in nxt dc, ch 3, sc in nxt dc, ch 1; sk 4 scallops and 1 dc, sc in sl st at beg of row, ch 3, sl st in nxt sc and sp—8 sp at waist including two ch-1 sps under arms.

Row 7: Ch 4, dc in same sp, ch 1, dc in same sp, (ch 2, sk sp, in nxt sp make dc, ch 1, dc, ch 1, dc) 3 times, ch 2, sl st in 3rd ch and sp—4 sets of two ch-1 sps.

Row 8: Ch 4, dc in same sp, (ch 1, make "V" sp in nxt ch-1 sp, ch 2, make "V" sp in nxt ch-1 sp) 4 times, except instead of final "V" sp make sl st in 3rd ch.

Rows 9–11: Ch 4, dc in same sp, (make "V" sp in nxt two ch-1 sps, ch 2, make "V" sp in nxt ch-1 sp) 4 times except instead of final "V" sp make sl st in 3rd ch and sp—4 sets of 3 "V" sps per set.

Rows 12 & 13: Ch 4, dc in same sp, (dc in nxt sp, ch 2, dc in same sp; make "V" sp in nxt ch-1 sp; ch 2, "V" sp in nxt ch-1 sp) 4 times except instead of final "V" sp make sl st in 3rd ch and sp.

Row 14: Ch 4, dc in same sp, (in ch-2 sp make dc, ch 1, dc, ch 1, dc, ch 1, dc; "V" sp in nxt ch-1 sp; ch 2, "V" sp in nxt ch-1 sp) 4 times except instead of final "V" sp, sl st in 3rd ch.

Row 15: Sc in ch-1 sp, (in each of nxt 3 ch-1 sps make 3 dc; sc in nxt ch-1 sp; ch 3, sc in ch-2 sp, ch 3, sc in ch-1 sp) 4 times except instead of final sc make sl st in 1st sc. Finish.

Wings—Right

Row 1: Attach thread in row 5 ch-2 sp in center back of bodice. Ch 3, sc in row 4 in ch-2 sp. Ch 3, sc in row 3 dc to right. Ch 3, sc in row 2 in ch-2 sp to right of dc. Ch 3, sc in row 1 in ch-1 sp—4 ch-3 sps.

Row 2: Ch 6, turn. (In each sp make sc, ch 3) across; in last sp also make dc—5 sps.

Rows 3 & 4: As row 2—6 and 7 sp.

Row 5: Ch 6, turn. (In each sp make sc, ch 3) across except in nxt-to-last sp make sc, ch 2, dc in last sp—7 sps.

Row 6: Ch 3, turn. (In nxt ch-3 sp make sc, ch 3) across; in last sp also make dc—7 sps. Finish **right** wing here. Make **left** wing to correspond. **Do not** cut thread.

Wing Edging

Row 7: Ch 6, turn, (sc in nxt sp, in nxt sp make 4 dc) 5 times; sc in nxt 2 sps, sl st across to right wing; sc in row-1 sp of wing; (sc in nxt sp, in nxt sp make 4 dc) 5 times, sc in nxt sp, ch 6, sc in same sp—5 sets of 4 dc per wing. Finish.

To stiffen: Make a cone from index card to fit inside skirt. Tape to hold shape. Cover stiffening board and cone with plastic wrap. Saturate angel in fabric stiffener or a 2-to-1 solution of fresh white glue and water. Gently squeeze out excess. Insert cone in skirt. Shape shoulders and wings. Lay angel on back with wings pinned flat on stiffening board until **almost** dry. Remove pins and cone. Pull wings up and out. Shape skirt so angel stands. Let dry. Trim with baubles, beads, bows, blossoms, or other decorations as desired. Bring ends of mono-filament together, and tie a knot in monofilament ends to form hanger. Tack at top center of ornament.

Ecru Embroidery

Delicate, ecru-on-ecru embroidery, worked in traditional holiday motifs, conveys understated elegance in this quartet of lace-trimmed ornaments. Finished by machine using French-sewing techniques, these lovely pieces will grace your seasonal decorating with unforgettable style.

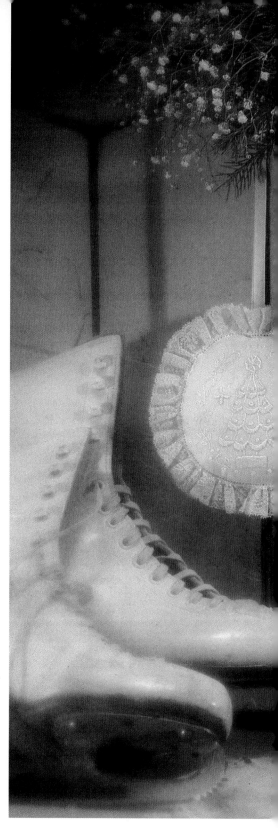

DMC	Color
ecru	ecru

Fabric: ecru Swiss batiste
Design size:

Holly & *Poinsettia*	2½" x 2½"
Tree	3¼" x 3"
Noel	3⅛" x 3⅛"

Note: Baste lining fabric to batiste before stitching.

Holly
- ⊜ Work padded satin stitch using one strand of floss.
- ⌇ Work stem stitch using one strand of floss.
- ● Work French knot using two strands of floss and wrapping floss around needle once.
- ↩ Work lazy-daisy stitch using two strands of floss.
- ⊘ Work two bullion knots close together, using one strand of floss.

Poinsettia
- ⊜ Work padded satin stitch using one strand of floss.
- O Work French knot using two strands of floss and wrapping floss around needle twice.
- ☆ Work French knot using two strands of floss and wrapping floss around needle three times.
- ⌇ Work stem stitch using one strand of floss.
- ↩ Work lazy-daisy stitch along stems, using two strands of floss.
- ⊘ Work bullion knots for petals, using one strand of floss.

Tree
- ⊜ Work padded satin stitch using one strand of floss.
- ⌇ Work stem stitch using one strand of floss.

- O Work French knot using two strands of floss and wrapping floss around needle twice.
- ⊘ Work bullion knot for petals, using one strand of floss.
- ↩ Work lazy-daisy stitch along stems, using two strands of floss.
- ✺ Work buttonhole stitch using two strands of floss.

Noel
- ⊜ Work padded satin stitch using one strand of floss.
- ☆ Work French knot using two strands of floss and wrapping floss around needle three times.
- ⌇ Work stem stitch using one strand of floss.
- ↩ Work lazy-daisy stitch using two strands of floss.

Finishing instructions:
Materials:
¼ yd. 44/45"-wide ecru fabric (for backing)
¼ yd. 44/45"-wide ecru fabric (for lining)
32" length ⅝"-wide ecru lace trim (for **each** ornament)
13" length ecru entredeux (for **each** ornament)
1 yd. ¼"-wide ivory satin ribbon, cut into 9" lengths (for hangers)
Thread to match fabrics
Polyester filling
Water-soluble fabric-marking pen
Hand-sewing needle
Straight pins
Scissors   Sewing machine

1. Complete embroidery following instructions given.
2. Center ornament pattern, found on page **130,** atop stitched design and lightly mark around edge of pattern on stitched front. Remove pattern and make a second marking ¼" inside the first marking. Second marking is edge of ornament. Set aside.
3. Zigzag along one long edge of entredeux, using a tight tension to form a "roll". Trim away excess fabric from **this** long edge. Set aside. Sew a gathering thread along one long edge of lace, and gather lace to fit entredeux, arranging gathers evenly. Butt gathered edge of lace to edge of

"roll," and zigzag the two pieces together. Place assembled entredeux-and-lace ruffle atop right side of stitched front, placing edge of entredeux toward seam allowance of ornament and edge of lace toward center of ornament. Align edge of entredeux "ladder" with marked edge of ornament, and pin.

Option: If you prefer a simpler trimming method, substitute pre-gathered lace trim for entredeux-and-lace trim.

4. Sew entredeux to ornament front, and remove pins.

5. Place ornament front and backing with right sides together and pin. Sew assembled front and backing fabric together, using previous stitching line as a guide for stitching, being careful not to catch lace in stitching, and leaving an opening for turning. Turn right-side out and stuff moderately with polyester filling. Whipstitch opening closed.

6. Tie a knot in each ribbon end to prevent fraying. Fold length of ribbon in half to form hanging loop, and tack knotted ribbon ends neatly to back side of ornament, placing loop at top center of ornament.

TREE

HOLLY

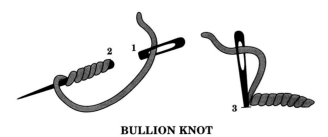

BULLION KNOT

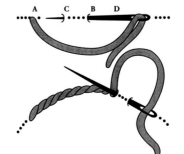

STEM STITCH

LAZY-DAISY STITCH

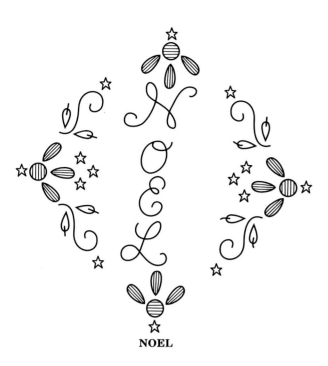

NOEL

POINSETTIA

PADDED SATIN STITCH

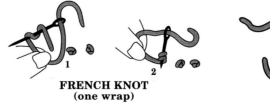

**FRENCH KNOT
(one wrap)**

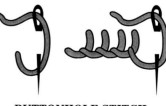

BUTTONHOLE STITCH

A Flurry of Snowflakes

Eight designs bring the magic of the season indoors with this gentle blizzard of crochet snowflakes. Shown here worked in ecru with gold highlights and white with silver highlights, and on page 33 in plain white, these pieces show the versatility of using a variety of fibers to create a completely different look using the same patterns. These gently falling charmers will make lovely package tags that become a splendid part of the gift.

Crochet Abbreviations and Terms:
beg—beginning
bet—between
ch—chain stitch
dc—double crochet
hdc—half double crochet
lp(s)—loop(s)
nxt—next
rep(s)—repeat(s)
rnd(s)—round(s)
sc—single crochet
sk—skip
sl st—slip stitch
sp(s)—space(s)
st(s)—stitch(es)

Beg shell: In specified sp or st work [ch 3 (counts as first dc), 2 dc, ch 3, 3 dc].
Shell: In specified sp or st work (3 dc, ch 3, 3 dc).

Gold Metallic Snowflakes
Materials:
Coats & Clark Knit-Cro-Sheen, ecru, size 10, 20 yards per ornament
FibreCraft non-elastic metallic thread, No. 3354, 2-ply, gold, 60-yd. spool (will make all 4 ornaments)
8" length ⅛"-wide metallic-gold cord for **each** ornament (for hanger)
Size 1/B (2.25mm) aluminum crochet hook **or** size needed to obtain gauge
Fabric stiffener

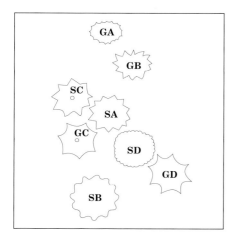

Gauge: Rnds 1 and 2 of *Snowflake A* = 1" diameter

Size: Each ornament = 3½"–4½" diameter

Note: Work each snowflake using one strand of metallic thread and one strand of ecru thread held together.

Snowflake A (GA)
Ch 6, sl st to beg ch to form a ring.
Rnd 1: Ch 1, work 12 sc in ring; sl st to beg sc.
Rnd 2: Ch 1, 2 sc in each sc around; sl st to beg sc—24 sc.
Rnd 3: Ch 1, sc in same st as joining; * ch 4, sk 1 st, sc in nxt sc; rep from * around, ending ch 4, sl st to beg sc—12 ch-4 sps.
Rnd 4: Sl st to first ch-4 sp, ch 1, 3 sc in same sp; * ch 5, 3 sc in nxt ch-4 sp; rep from * around, ending ch 2, dc in beg sc.
Rnd 5: Ch 1, sc in last lp formed; * ch 7, sc in nxt ch-5 sp; rep from * around, ending ch 7; sl st to beg sc.
Rnd 6: Ch 1, sc in same st as joining; * (3 sc, ch 3, 3 sc) in nxt ch-7 sp **, sc in nxt sc; rep from * around, ending at **; sl st to beg sc.
Rnd 7: * Ch 2, sk 1 sc, sl st in nxt sc, ch 2, sk 1 sc, (sl st, ch 4, sl st) in ch-3 sp, (ch 2, sk 1 sc, sl st in nxt sc) twice **, ch 2, sk 1 sc, sl st in nxt sc; rep from * around, ending at **, ch 2, sl st in beg sl st. Fasten off.
Finishing: Weave in ends. Stiffen and block if needed. Bring ends of cord together, and tie a knot in cord ends to form hanger. Insert loop end through any ch-4 sp of Rnd 7.

Snowflake B (GB)
Ch 6, sl st to beg ch to form a ring.
Rnd 1: Ch 1, (sc in ring, ch 4) 6 times, sl st to beg sc—6 ch-4 sps.
Rnd 2: Ch 5 (counts as first dc and ch 2), sc in nxt ch-3 sp; * ch 2, dc in nxt sc, ch 2, sc in nxt ch-3 sp; rep from *

around, ending ch 2, sl st to top of 3rd ch of beg ch-5.
Rnd 3: Ch 1, sc in same st as joining; * 2 sc in nxt ch-2 sp **, sc in nxt st; rep from * around, ending at **; sl st to beg sc.
Rnd 4: Ch 1, sc in same st as joining; * ch 3, sk 2 sc, sc in nxt sc; rep from * around, ending ch 3, sl st to beg sc—12 ch-3 sps.
Rnd 5: Sl st to first ch-3 sp, ch 3 (counts as first dc), in same sp work (dc, ch 2, 2 dc); * (2 dc, ch 2, 2 dc) in nxt ch-3 sp; rep from * around; sl st to top of beg ch-3.
Rnd 6: Sl st to first ch-2 sp, ch 1, sc in same sp; * ch 5, sc in nxt ch-2 sp; rep from * around, ending ch 5; sl st to beg sc.
Rnd 7: Ch 1, sc in same st as joining; * ch 2, in nxt ch-5 sp work (sc, ch 3, sc, ch 5, sc, ch 3, sc), ch 2 **, sc in nxt sc; rep from * around, ending at **; sl st to beg sc. Fasten off.
Finishing: Weave in ends. Stiffen and block if needed. Bring ends of cord together, and tie a knot in cord ends to form hanger. Insert loop end through any ch-5 sp of Rnd 7.

Snowflake C (GC)
Ch 8, sl st to beg ch to form a ring.
Rnd 1: Ch 3 (counts as first dc), work 21 dc in ring; sl st to top of beg ch-3—22 dc.
Rnd 2: Ch 1, sc in same st as joining; * ch 5, sk 2 dc, sc in nxt dc; rep from * around, ending ch 5, sk 2 dc, sl st to beg sc—7 ch-5 sps.
Rnd 3: Ch 1, sc in same st as joining; * ch 7, sc in nxt sc; rep from * around, ending ch 7; sl st to beg sc.
Rnd 4: Ch 1, sc in same st as joining; * 7 sc in nxt ch-7 sp, sc in nxt sc; rep from * around, ending 7 sc in ch-7 sp; sl st to beg sc.
Rnd 5: Ch 1, sc in same st as joining; * ch 3, sk 3 sc, (sc, ch 3, sc) in nxt sc, ch 3, sk 3 sc **, sc in nxt sc; rep from * around, ending at **; sl st to beg sc.
Rnd 6: Ch 1, sc in same st as joining; * ch 4, sk ch-3 sp, (sc, ch 3, sc) in nxt ch-3 sp,

ch 4, sk ch-3 sp **, sc in nxt sc; rep from * around, ending at **; sl st to beg sc.

Rnd 7: Ch 1, (sc, ch 3, sc) in same st as joining; * ch 3, sk ch-4 sp, in nxt ch-3 sp work (sc, ch 3, sc, ch 5, sc, ch 3, sc), ch 3, sk ch-4 sp **, (sc, ch 3, sc) in nxt sc; rep from * around, ending at **; sl st to beg sc. Fasten off.

Finishing: Weave in ends. Stiffen and block if needed. Bring ends of cord together, and tie a knot in cord ends to form hanger. Insert loop end through any ch-5 sp of Rnd 7.

Snowflake D (GD)
Ch 4, sl st to beg ch to form a ring.

Rnd 1: Ch 1, work 8 sc in ring; sl st to beg sc.

Rnd 2: Ch 1, sc in same st as joining; * ch 1 , sc in nxt sc; rep from * around, ending ch 1; sl st to beg sc.

Rnd 3: Ch 1, sc in same st as joining; * ch 3, sk ch-1 sp, sc in nxt sc; rep from * around, ending ch 3, sk ch-1 sp; sl st to beg sc.

Rnd 4: Ch 1, sc in same st as joining; * ch 5, sk ch-3 sp, sc in nxt sc; rep from * around, ending ch 2, dc in beg sc to join.

Rnd 5: Ch 1, sc in last lp formed; * ch 6, sc in nxt ch-5 sp; rep from * around, ending ch 6; sl st to beg sc.

Rnd 6: Ch 1, sc in same st as joining; * in nxt ch-6 sp work (hdc, 2 dc, ch 3, 2 dc, hdc) **, sc in nxt sc; rep from * around, ending at **; sl st to beg sc.

Rnd 7: Ch 1, sc in each st around, working (sc, ch 3, sc) in each ch-3 sp; sl st to beg sc.

Rnd 8: Ch 1, (sc, ch 2, sc) in same st as joining; * ch 3, sk 4 sc, in ch-3 sp work (sc, ch 3, sc, ch 7, sc, ch 3, sc), ch 3, sk 4 sc **, in nxt sc work (sc, ch 2, sc); rep from * around, ending at **; sl st to beg sc. Fasten off.

Finishing: Weave in ends. Stiffen and block if needed. Bring ends of cord together, and tie a knot in cord ends to form hanger. Insert loop end through any ch-7 sp of Rnd 8.

Silver Metallic Snowflakes
Materials:
Coats & Clark Knit-Cro-Sheen, Art. A-64M, white/silver, size 10, one ball (will make all four snowflakes)
8" length ⅛"-wide metallic-silver cord for **each** ornament (for hanger)
Size 7 (1.5mm) steel crochet hook **or** size needed to obtain gauge
Fabric stiffener
Gauge: Rnds 1 and 2 of *Snowflake A* = 1" diameter

Size: Each ornament = 4"–4½" diameter

Snowflake A (SA)
Ch 6, sl st to beg ch to form a ring.

Rnd 1: Ch 1, work 12 sc in ring; sl st to beg sc.

Rnd 2: Ch 1, sc in same st as joining; * ch 5, sk 1 sc, sc in nxt sc; rep from * around, ending ch 5, sk 1 sc, sl st to beg sc—6 ch-5 sps.

Rnd 3: Ch 1, sc in same st as joining; * 5 sc in nxt ch-5 sp, sc in nxt sc; rep from * around, ending 5 sc in ch-5 sp; sl st to beg sc.

Rnd 4: Ch 1, (sc, ch 3, sc) in same sc as joining; * ch 3, sk 2 sc, (sc, ch 3, sc) in nxt sc; rep from * around, ending ch 3, sk 2 sc; sl st to beg sc.

Rnd 5: Sl st to first ch-3 sp, ch 1, (sc, ch 3, sc) in same sp; * ch 2, sc in nxt ch-3 sp, ch 2 **, (sc, ch 3, sc) in nxt ch-3 sp; rep from * around, ending at **; sl st to beg sc.

Rnd 6: Sl st to first ch-3 sp, ch 1, sc in same sp; * ch 5, sc in nxt ch-3 sp; rep from * around, ending ch 5, sl st to beg sc.

Rnd 7: Rep Rnd 3.

Rnd 8: Ch 1, sc in same st as joining; * ch 1, sk 2 sc, shell in nxt sc, ch 1, sk 2 sc **, sc in nxt sc; rep from * around, ending at **, sl st to beg sc.

Rnd 9: Ch 1, (sc, ch 3, sc) in same sc as joining; * ch 3, in ch-3 sp of nxt shell work (sc, ch 3, sc, ch 5, sc, ch 3, sc), ch 3 **, (sc, ch 3, sc) in nxt sc; rep from * around, ending at **; sl st to beg sc. Fasten off.

Finishing: Weave in ends. Stiffen and block if needed. Bring ends of cord together, and tie a knot in cord ends to form hanger. Insert loop end through any ch-5 sp of Rnd 9.

Snowflake B (SB)
Ch 4, sl st to beg ch to form a ring.

Rnd 1: Ch 3 (counts as first dc), work 11 dc in ring; sl st to top of beg ch-3—12 dc.

Rnd 2: Ch 1, sc in same st as joining; * ch 3, sc in nxt dc; rep from * around, ending ch 1, hdc in beg sc to join—12 ch-3 sps.

Rnd 3: Ch 1, sc in last lp formed; * ch 3, sc in nxt sp; rep from * around, ending ch 3, sl st to beg sc.

Rnd 4: Sl st in nxt ch-3 sp, ch 3 (counts as first dc), 2 dc in same sp; * ch 2, 3 dc in nxt ch-3 sp; rep from * around, ending ch 2; sl st to top of beg ch-3.

Rnd 5: Sl st in nxt dc, ch 1, (sc, ch 3, sc) in same st; * 5 dc in nxt ch-2 sp, sk nxt dc, (sc, ch 3, sc) in nxt dc, sk nxt dc; rep from * around, ending 5 dc in ch-2 sp; sl st to beg sc.

Rnd 6: Sl st in first ch-3 sp, ch 3 (counts as first dc), 4 dc in same sp; * ch 1, sk 2 dc, sc in nxt dc, ch 1, sk 2 dc **, 5 dc in ch-3 sp; rep from * around, ending at **; sl st to top of beg ch-3.

Rnd 7: Ch 1, sc in each st and ch-1 sp around, working 3 sc in center dc of each 5-dc group, sl st to beg sc.

Rnd 8: Sl st to center sc of 3-sc group, ch 1, (sc, ch 3, sc) in same sc; * ch 3, sk 4 sc, sc in nxt sc, ch 3, sk 4 sc **, (sc, ch 3, sc) in nxt sc (center sc of 3-sc group); rep from * around, ending at **; sl st to beg sc.

Rnd 9: Sl st in ch-3 sp, ch 1, in same sp work [(sc, ch 3) 3 times, sc]; * ch 2, sk 1 sc, (sc, ch 3, sc) in nxt sc, ch 2 **, in nxt ch-3 sp work [(sc, ch 3) 3 times, sc]; rep from * around, ending at **; sl st to beg sc. Fasten off.

Finishing: Weave in ends. Stiffen and block if needed. Bring ends of cord together, and tie a knot in cord ends to form hanger. Insert loop end through any ch-3 sp of Rnd 9.

Snowflake C (SC)
Ch 8, sl st to beg ch to form a ring.

Rnd 1: Ch 1, work 16 sc in ring; sl st to beg sc.

Rnd 2: Ch 1, sc in same st as joining; * 3 dc in nxt sc, sc in nxt sc; rep from * around, working 3 dc in last sc; sl st to beg sc.

Rnd 3: Ch 3 (counts as first dc); * sk 1 dc, in nxt dc work (2 dc, ch 2, 2 dc), sk nxt dc **, dc in sc; rep from * around, ending at **; sl st to top of beg ch-3.

Rnd 4: Sl st to first ch-2 sp, work beg shell in same sp; * sk nxt 2 dc, dc in nxt dc, shell in nxt ch-2 sp; rep from * around, ending dc in nxt dc; sl st to top of beg ch-3.

Rnd 5: Ch 5 (counts as first dc and ch 2); * shell in ch-3 sp of nxt shell, ch 2 **, sk nxt 3 dc, dc in nxt dc, ch 2; rep from * around, ending at **; sl st to 3rd ch of beg ch-5.

Rnd 6: Ch 1, sc in same st as joining; * 2 sc in ch-2 sp, sc in 3 dc, in ch-3 sp work (sc, ch 5, sc), sc in 3 dc, 2 sc in ch-2 sp **, sc in dc; rep from * around, ending at **; sl st to beg sc.

Rnd 7: Ch 1, (sc, ch 3, sc) in same st as joining; * ch 3, sk 3 sc, sc in nxt sc, ch 3, sk 2 sc, in ch-5 sp work (sc, ch 3, sc, ch 5, sc, ch 3, sc), ch 3, sk 2 sc, sc in nxt sc, ch 3, sk 3 sc **, (sc, ch 3, sc) in nxt sc; rep from * around, ending at **; sl st to beg sc. Fasten off.

Finishing: Weave in ends. Stiffen and block if needed. Bring ends of cord together, and tie a knot in cord ends to

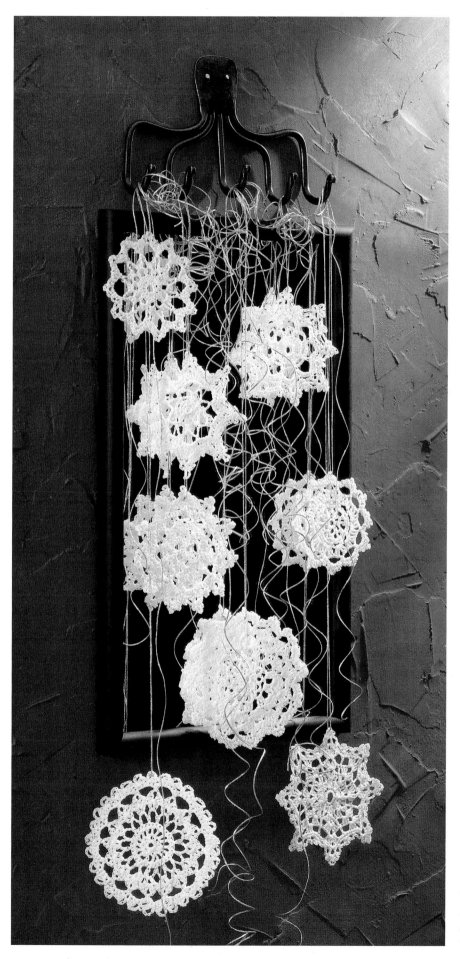

form hanger. Insert loop end through any ch-5 sp of Rnd 9.

Snowflake D (SD)
Ch 5, sl st to beg ch to form a ring.

Rnd 1: Ch 1, (sc in ring, ch 3) 8 times; sl st to beg sc—8 ch-3 sps.

Rnd 2: Ch 4 (counts as first dc and ch 1); * dc in nxt ch-3 sp, ch 1 **, dc in nxt sc, ch 1; rep from * around, ending at **; sl st to 3rd ch of beg ch-4—16 ch-1 sps.

Rnd 3: Ch 1, sc in each dc and ch-1 sp around; sl st to beg sc—32 sts.

Rnd 4: Ch 1, sc in same st as joining; * ch 5, sk 1 sc, sc in nxt sc; rep from * around, ending ch 2, dc in beg sc to join—16 ch-5 sps.

Rnd 5: Ch 1, (sc, ch 3, sc) in last lp formed; * ch 3, (sc, ch 3, sc) in nxt ch-5 sp; rep from * around, ending ch 1, hdc in beg sc to join.

Rnd 6: Ch 1, sc in last lp formed; * (2 dc, ch 2, 2 dc) in nxt ch-3 sp **, sc in nxt ch-3 sp; rep from * around, ending at **; sl st to beg sc.

Rnd 7: Sl st to first ch-2 sp, ch 1, sc in same sp; * ch 5, sc in nxt ch-2 sp; rep from * around, ending ch 5, sl st to beg sc.

Rnd 8: Ch 1, sc in same st as joining; * 5 sc in nxt ch-5 sp, sc in nxt sc; rep from * around, ending 5 sc in ch-5 sp; sl st to beg sc.

Rnd 9: (Ch 5, 2 dc) in same st as joining; * sk 2 sc, (sl st, ch 5, 2 dc) in nxt sc; rep from * around, ending sk 2 sc, sl st in beg sl st. Fasten off.

Finishing: Weave in ends. Stiffen and block if needed. Bring ends of cord together, and tie a knot in cord ends to form hanger. Insert loop end through any ch-5 sp of Rnd 9.

White Thread Snowflakes
Materials:
One 50-gram ball DMC Cébélia® cotton crochet thread, white, size 10 (will make all eight snowflakes)
Kreinik Balger medium (#16) braid, color: 102 Vatican (for hangers)
Size 7 (1.5mm) aluminum crochet hook **or** size needed to obtain gauge
Fabric stiffener

Gauge: Rnds 1 and 2 of *Snowflake A* = 1" diameter

Size: Each ornament = 3½"–4½" diameter

Work snowflakes as for *Gold Metallic Snowflakes* and *Silver Metallic Snowflakes,* using one strand of cotton crochet thread.

An English Country Christmas

From breathtaking needlepoint to charming cross stitch and whimsical knitting, there is something on the following pages for everyone who loves decorating for the holidays with a hint of English-country appeal. Whether you prefer the gorgeous Needlepoint Angel, Bell, Rocking Horse, and Sleigh *ornaments, the equestrian-inspired* To the Hunt *ornaments, or the adorable* Knitted Christmas Ornaments, *which are displayed on an unusual bare-branched tree, you're certain to find an assortment of delights for your holiday wonderment.*

Needlepoint Angel, Bell, Horse, and Sleigh

Needlepoint, worked on 18-mesh canvas using a single strand of yarn, was used to portray these classic holiday motifs. Finished as small ornaments, these pieces will allow you to decorate for the season in unforgettable style. For added variety that creates a completely different look, stitch your favorite on another count mesh. The sleigh ornament, right, and pillow, below, provide a wonderful example of the variation that can be achieved.

Paternayan	Color
✳ 200	steel gray, dk.
‖ 202	steel gray, med.
∕ 203	steel gray, lt.
■ 221	charcoal gray
• 260	white
▲ 440	golden brown, dk.
ɑ 493	peach flesh
✗ 500	federal blue, dk.
⊕ 504	federal blue, med.
∟ 505	federal blue, lt.

	506	federal blue, vy. lt.
ı	660	pine green, vy. dk.
⅍	661	pine green, dk.
⅄	662	pine green, med.
ℓ	693	loden green, med.
ⱱ	700	butterscotch, dk.
ℭ	702	butterscotch, med.
ⱦ	731	honey gold, dk.
ꙅ	953	strawberry, med.
•	968	Christmas red, dk.
•	970	Christmas red, med.

Fabric: 18-mesh white mono-deluxe canvas from Zweigart®

Stitch count: 46H x 46W

Design size: 2½" x 2½"

Instructions: Work design in tent stitch in basketweave method, using one strand of yarn.

Option: These designs can be worked on a lower-count canvas to make them larger—ideal for small pillows. Use an 8½" square of 10-mesh canvas for **each** pillow. Work design in tent stitch using three strands of yarn. Finish as desired.

General materials:
Thread to match fabric
Polyester filling
Scissors
Sewing machine
Iron

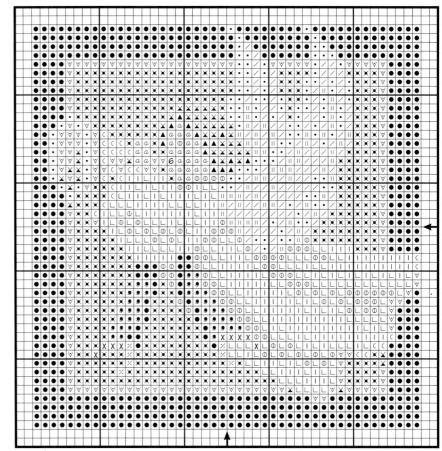

ANGEL

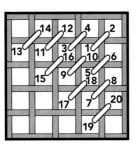

**TENT STITCH
BASKETWEAVE
METHOD**

ROCKING HORSE

Finishing materials for ornaments:
3½" square fabric for backing (for **each** ornament)
8½" length gold cording (for **each** ornament)

Finishing: Turn to page **131** for "Basic Ornament-Finishing Instructions."

Finishing materials for pillow:
8½" square muslin (for **each** pillow)
⅜ yd. 44"-wide dark-blue acetate satin
Two 25m skeins size 5 DMC pearl cotton, color: 729 gold

1. Cut one 3"-wide strip across width of blue satin. Cut a second 3"-wide strip 20" long. Sew short ends of strips together, forming one continuous loop. Divide loop into quarters, marking divisions on wrong side. Sew a gathering stitch ¼" from each long edge.
2. Baste needlepoint square to muslin square around outer edges.
3. Gather one edge of satin strip. Pin around edges of needlepoint, placing right sides of fabric together. (**Note:** Line of gathering stitching should lie along outermost row of stitched area.)

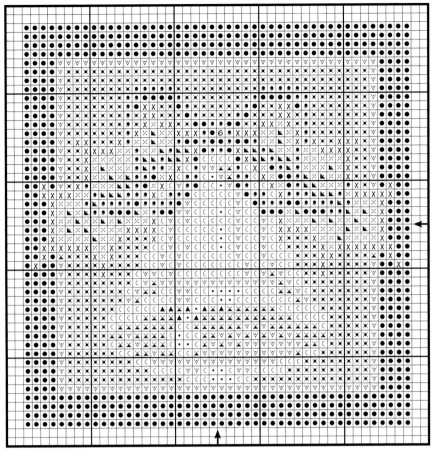

BELL

Baste through all layers along gathering line; sew along same line. Trim canvas ½" from stitching. Press gathered satin strip away from needlepoint.

4. Smooth gathered satin strip outward, pulling gathering thread along outer edge to fit muslin square. Pin in place, rounding corners if desired. Hand baste along outer edge. Sew in place ½" from raw edges. Trim corners if rounded.

5. Cut out pillow back, using front as a pattern. Sew pillow front to pillow back, placing right sides of fabric together, using a ½" seam allowance, and leaving an opening for turning. Turn right-side out. Stuff with polyester filling and whipstitch opening closed.

6. Turn to page **141** for "How-Tos for Making Twisted Cording." Whipstitch cording to pillow front along edge of needlepoint insert, beginning and ending in a corner.

7. Turn to page **101** for tassel-making instructions. Use a 2" card, and make four tassels. Sew tops of tassels to corners of pillow.

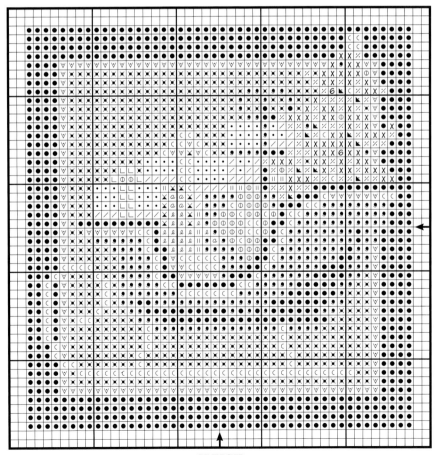

SLEIGH

Needlepoint Violin, Horn, and Drum

Rich, vibrant colors make this trio of musical-instrument orna-ments "sing" from the branches of your Christmas tree. The ornaments pictured on the opposite page are worked in needle-point. But they are equally lovely when done in counted cross stitch, as shown below. Stitch this threesome to grace the branches of your own tree, or choose an appropriate design to present to the music fan you know.

DMC Laine Colbert	DMC	Color
ecru	ecru	ecru (five skeins)
∕ noir	310	black
• 7107	304	red
+ 7108	498	red, dk.
= 7110	815	garnet
Z 7385	3345	forest, vy. dk.
C 7455	437	tan, lt.
▲ 7479	433	brown, med.
○ 7485	680	old gold, dk.
⊗ 7489	898	coffee brown, vy. dk.
‖ 7504	676	old gold, lt.
S 7845	434	brown, lt.
T 7846	435	tan
< 7905	745	old gold, vy. lt.
X 7909	910	jade, med.

	DMC	Color
b/ss	310	black
ss	319	pistachio, vy. dk.
bs	434	brown, lt.
ss	502	blue green
b/ss	898	coffee brown, vy. dk.

Kreinik Fine Braid #8
002HL   gold hi-luster

Fabric: 12-mesh white mono-deluxe canvas from Zweigart®

Stitch count:
Violin	40H x 47W
Horn	37H x 37W
Drum	39H x 59W

Design size:
Violin	3⅞" x 3⅜"
Horn	3⅛" x 3⅛"
Drum	3½" x 5⅛"

Instructions: Work design in tent stitch in basketweave method, using two strands of wool. Work background in ecru, using two strands of wool and stitching to outer border of chart. Back-stitch (bs) using two strands of floss. Straight stitch (ss) using two strands of floss unless otherwise indicated.

Backstitch (bs) instructions:

Violin
434	pine branches
310	sounding-board holes

Horn
434	pine branches
898	horn

Drum
434	pine branches
898	pinecones on left

Straight-stitch (ss) instructions:

Violin
310	strings
502	pine needles on either side of violin center and at far lower right
319	remainder of pine needles

Horn
502	pine needles at left and bottom right
319	remainder of pine needles

Drum
002HL	drum ropes (one strand)
898	drumsticks
319	pine needles at top right, bottom right, and middle left
502	remainder of pine needles

Finishing materials:
¼ yd. 44"-wide red-print fabric (for backing)

One skein **each** size 5 DMC pearl cotton, colors: 816 red, 986 green

Finishing:
Turn to page **131** for "Basic Orna-ment-Finishing Instructions."

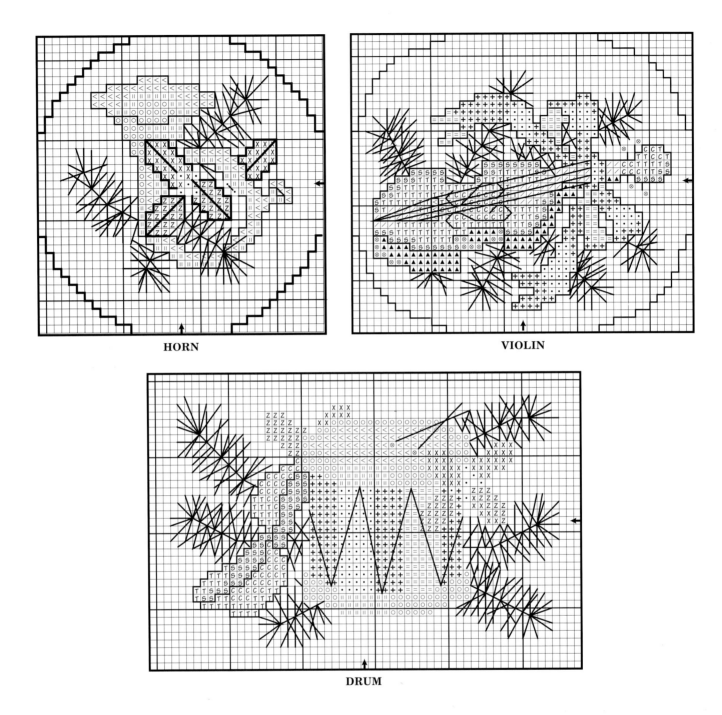

HORN

VIOLIN

DRUM

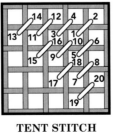

TENT STITCH
BASKETWEAVE
METHOD

Knitted Christmas Ornaments

Tiny, knitted treasures make fantastic adornments for a miniature tree such as the one shown here. Use this tiny delight to deck your foyer or kitchen in holiday style. Or give these ornaments to a college student or someone else whose living space limits them to using a small, tabletop tree to mark the season.

Knitting Abbreviations and Terms:

bo—bind off

co—cast on

inc—increase

k—knit

k 2 tog—k 2 sts tog

k inc—k in front and back of same st

nxt—next

p—purl

p 2 sso—pass 2 slipped sts over last knitted st

p 2 tog-b—insert needle through back of nxt 2 sts and then purl them tog

p inc—p in front and back of same st

rem—remain(ing)

RS—right side

sl—slip

ssk—insert needle in front of first st and in back of nxt st and k these 2 sts tog

st(s)—stitch(es)

tog—together

WS—wrong side

yo—yarn over

Note: Dk-weight yarn is between sport-weight yarn and worsted-weight yarn.

Santa

Materials:

Small amounts dk-weight yarn, colors:
  ecru (A), beige (B), red (C)

One pair size 5 (3.75mm) knitting needles

Size 6/G (4.25mm) crochet hook

One ½" gold jingle bell

12" length 6-strand black embroidery floss

Tapestry needle
Size: Approximately 5" long

With A, co 2 sts.
Row 1: K.
Rows 2 & 4: P.
Row 3: K inc in 2 sts—4 sts.
Row 5: K 1, k inc in nxt 2 sts, k 1—6 sts.
Row 6: P 1, p inc, p 2, p inc, p 1—8 sts.
Row 7: (K 2, k inc) twice, k 2—10 sts.
Row 8: P 2, p inc, p 4, p inc, p 2—12 sts.
Row 9: K 3, k inc, k 4, k inc, k 3—14 sts.
Row 10: P 3, p inc, p 6, p inc, p 3—16 sts.
Row 11: K 4, k inc, k 6, k inc, k 4—18 sts.
Row 12: P 4, p inc, p 8, p inc, p 4—20 sts.
Row 13: K 5, k inc, k 8, k inc, k 5—22 sts.
Row 14: P 5, p inc, p 10, p inc, p 5—24 sts.
Row 15: K 6, k inc, k 10, k inc, k 6—26 sts.
Row 16: P 6, p inc, p 12, p inc, p 6—28 sts.
Rows 17, 19, & 21: With B, k.
Rows 18, 20, & 22: P.
Rows 23–28: With A, k.
Row 29: With C, k.
Row 30: P.
Row 31: K 6, ssk, k 12, k 2 tog, k 6—26 sts.
Rows 32, 34, 36, & 38: P.
Row 33: K 5, ssk, k 12, k 2 tog, k 5—24 sts.
Row 35: K 5, ssk, k 10, k 2 tog, k 5—22 sts.
Row 37: K 4, ssk, k 10, k 2 tog, k 4—20 sts.
Row 39: K 4, ssk, k 8, k 2 tog, k 4—18 sts.
Row 40: P 4, p 2 tog, p 6, p 2 tog-b, p 4—16 sts.
Row 41: K 3, ssk, k 6, k 2 tog, k 3—14 sts.
Row 42: P 3, p 2 tog, p 4, p 2 tog-b, p 3—12 sts.
Row 43: K 2, ssk, k 4, k 2 tog, k 2—10 sts.
Row 44: P 2, p 2 tog, p 2, p 2 tog-b, p 2—8 sts.
Row 45: K 1, ssk, k 2, k 2 tog, k 1—6 sts.
Row 46: P 1, p 2 tog, p 2 tog-b, p 1—4 sts.
Row 47: Ssk, k 2 tog—2 sts.
Row 48: P 2 tog—1 st.
Bo all sts.

Finishing:
1. Work two eyes in backstitch, using tapestry needle and six strands black embroidery floss and spacing ⅝" apart. With two strands A, work

mustache between and under eyes in an inverted "V" shape.
2. Weave in all ends. Sew back seam. Attach jingle bell at tip of hat. Fold hat down and toward front ¾", folding in a diagonal line. Tack in place, using C.
3. Attach C at center top of hat, using crochet hook. Ch 10 and sl st in same place where you first attached C. Fasten off and weave in ends.

Red-and-White Stocking
Materials:
Small amounts dk-weight yarn, colors: ecru (A), red (B)
One pair size 5 (3.75mm) knitting needles
Size 6/G (4.25mm) crochet hook
Tapestry needle
Stitch holder

Size: Approximately 3½" long

With A, co 18 sts.
Cuff—Rows 1–6: K.
Leg—Row 7: With B, k.
Row 8: P.
Rep Rows 7 and 8 until 1¾" from beg, ending after Row 8.
First Half of Heel—Row 1 (RS): With A, k 5; turn, leaving rem sts unworked.
Row 2: Sl 1, p 4.
Rep Rows 1 and 2 twice more.
Short Rows: K 2, k 2 tog, k 1, turn; sl 1, p 3, turn; k 1, k 2 tog, k 1, turn; p 3 tog; leave rem st on holder.
Second Half—Row 1 (WS): Slip sts to right-hand needle and turn to work a WS row. With A, p 5; turn, leaving rem sts unworked.
Row 2: Sl 1, k 4.
Rep Rows 1 and 2 twice more.
Short Rows: P 2, p 2 tog, p 1, turn; sl 1, k 3, turn; p 1, p 2 tog, p 1, turn; k 3 tog; turn.
Foot—Row 1 (WS): With B, p 1 from needle, pick up and p 4 sts on side of heel, p across 8 sts from instep, pick up and p 4 sts on side of heel, p 1 from holder—18 sts.
Rows 2 & 4: K.
Rows 3 & 5: P.
Row 6: * K 1, k 2 tog; rep from * across—12 sts.
Row 7: P.
Rows 8 & 10: With A, k.
Rows 9 & 11: P.
Row 12: K 2 tog across—6 sts. Cut yarn, leaving a 6" tail.

Finishing:
1. Thread tail through rem sts and pull tightly to close tip, using tapestry needle.
2. Weave in all ends. Sew back seam.
3. Attach A at back seam, using crochet hook. Ch 10 and sl st in same place where you first attached A. Fasten off and weave in ends.

Striped Sock
Materials:
Small amounts dk-weight yarn, colors: dark green (A), red (B), ecru (C)
One pair size 5 (3.75mm) knitting needles
Size 6/G (4.25mm) crochet hook
Tapestry needle
Stitch holder

Size: Approximately 3½" long

With A, co 18 sts.
Cuff—Rows 1 & 2: K 1, p 1.
Leg—Row 3: With B, k.
Row 4: P.
Rows 5 & 6: Rep Rows 3 and 4 with C.
Rows 7 & 8: Rep Rows 3 and 4 with A.
Rows 9–14: Rep Rows 3–8.
First Half of Heel— Row 1 (RS): With A, k 5; turn, leaving rem sts unworked.
Row 2: Sl 1, p 4.
Rep Rows 1 and 2 twice more.
Short Rows: K 2, k 2 tog, k 1, turn; sl 1, p 3, turn; k 1, k 2 tog, k 1, turn; p 3 tog; leave rem st on holder.
Second Half—Row 1 (WS): Slip sts to right-hand needle and turn to work a WS row. With A, p 5; turn, leaving rem sts unworked.
Row 2: Sl 1, k 4.
Rep Rows 1 and 2 twice more.
Short Rows: P 2, p 2 tog, p 1, turn; sl 1, k 3, turn; p 1, p 2 tog, p 1, turn; k 3 tog; turn.
Foot—Row 1 (WS): With B, p 1 from needle, pick up and p 4 sts on side of heel, p across 8 sts from instep, pick up and p 4 sts on side of heel, p 1 from holder—18 sts.
Row 2: K.
Row 3: With C, p.
Row 4: K.
Row 5: With A, p.
Row 6: With A, * k 1, k 2 tog; rep from * across—12 sts.
Row 7: With B, p.
Row 8: K.
Rows 9 & 10: Rep Rows 3 and 4.
Row 11: Rep Row 5.

Row 12: K 2 tog across—6 sts. Cut yarn, leaving a 6" tail.

Finishing:
1. Thread tail through rem sts and pull tightly to close tip, using tapestry needle.
2. Weave in all ends. Sew back seam.
3. Attach A at back seam, using crochet hook. Ch 10 and sl st in same place where you first attached A. Fasten off and weave in ends.

Lacy Angel
Materials:
Small amount dk-weight yarn, color: ecru
2 yds. gold #16 braid
One pair size 5 (3.75mm) knitting needles
Size 6/G (4.25mm) crochet hook
Tapestry needle   Cotton ball

Size: Approximately 3"

Co 25 sts.
Row 1 & all WS Rows: P.
Row 2: K 1; * yo, ssk, k 1, k 2 tog, yo, k 1; rep from * across.
Row 4: K 2; * yo, sl 2 knitwise, k 1, p 2 sso, yo, k 3; rep from * across, end last rep with k 2 instead of k 3.
Rep Rows 1–4 twice more.
Neck Shaping—Rows 1, 3, & 5, (WS): P.
Row 2: (K 2 tog) twice, k 3 tog to end of row—9 sts.
Row 3: P.
Row 4: * k inc **, k 1; rep from * across, end at **—14 sts.
Row 6: K.
Row 7: P.
Row 8: K 2 tog across—7 sts. Cut yarn, leaving an 8" tail.

Finishing:
1. Thread tail through rem sts and pull tightly to close tip, using tapestry needle.
2. Weave in all ends. Insert cotton ball into head area. Sew back seam.
3. Cut 12" length of braid, wrap around neck twice, and tie securely in bow at front.
Wings: Wrap braid five times around width of four fingers. Wrap ends around center of these loops several times and tie ends together tightly. Attach at center back of neck.
Halo: Cut three 6½" lengths of braid. Knot one end. Work tog to form braid. Knot opposite end. Wrap around head, inserting knotted ends at center back

of head to secure in place. Attach yarn at top of head, using crochet hook. Ch 10 and sl st in same place where you first attached yarn. Fasten off and weave in ends.

Christmas Tree
Materials:
Small amount dk-weight yarn, color: dark green
12" length gold #16 braid
16" length red #16 braid
One pair size 5 (3.75mm) knitting needles
Size 6/G (4.25mm) crochet hook
Tapestry needle
Small gold star sequin

Size: Approximately 3"

Co 4 sts.
First Half—Rows 1–4: K.
Row 5: Co 6 sts at beg of row, k across 4 sts—10 sts.
Row 6: Co 6 sts at beg of row, p across 10 sts—16 sts.
Row 7: K.
Row 8 & all subsequent WS rows: P.
Row 9: K 2 tog, k to last 2 sts, ssk—14 sts.
Rep Rows 8 and 9 until 2 sts rem, ending after Row 8. Work 2 rows even.
Second Half—Row 1: K inc in 2 sts on needle—4 sts.
Row 2 & all WS rows: P.
Row 3: K inc in first st, k to last 2 sts, k inc in nxt st, k 1.
Rep Rows 2 and 3 until 16 sts are obtained, ending after Row 2. Work 2 rows even.
Lower Shaping: Bo 6 sts at beg of nxt 2 rows. K 4 rows on rem 4 sts. Bo all sts, leaving a 10" tail.

Finishing:
1. Hold both halves of tree tog and sew sides, using tapestry needle.
2. On one side of tree only, work two rows of zigzag in backstitch, using gold braid. Work French knots with red braid, wrapping braid around tapestry needle three times for each and positioning one knot in center opening of each "V" of zigzag rows.
3. Sew small sequin at center top.
4. Attach yarn at top of tree, using crochet hook. Ch 10 and sl st in same place where you first attached yarn. Fasten off and weave in ends.

Mittens
Materials:
Small amounts dk-weight yarn, colors: red (A), ecru (B)

One pair size 5 (3.75mm) knitting needles
Size 6/G (4.25mm) crochet hook
Tapestry needle

Size: Approximately 3"

Note: Make two mittens.

With A, co 12 sts.
Rows 1 & 2: * K 1, p 1; rep from * across.
Row 3: With B; * k inc, k 1; rep from * across—18 sts.
Row 4 & all subsequent WS Rows: P.
Row 5: K 1, k inc, k to last 3 sts, k inc, k 2—20 sts.
Row 7: K 2, k inc, k to last 4 sts, k inc, k 3—22 sts.
Row 9: K 3, k inc, k to last 5 sts, k inc, k 4—24 sts.
Row 11: K 4, k inc, k to last 6 sts, k inc, k 5—26 sts.
Row 12: P.
Right Half of Thumb—Row 1: K 5; turn, leaving rem sts unworked.
Row 2: P.
Row 3: K 2 tog, sl 1, k 2 tog, sl both sts from right-hand needle over st from left-hand needle. Bo rem st.
Left Half of Thumb—Row 1: Sl first 16 sts from left-hand needle to right-hand needle without knitting them, k 5.
Row 2: P 5, turn.
Row 3: Rep Row 3 of Right Half of Thumb.
Hand—Row 1 (RS): Sl 16 sts back to left-hand needle, with B, k 16.
Rows 2, 4 & 6: P.
Rows 3 & 5: K.
Rows 7 & 8: With A, rep Rows 3 and 4.
Row 9: K 2 tog, k 4, k 4 tog, k 4, k 2 tog—11 sts. Cut yarn, leaving a 6" tail.

Finishing:
1. Thread tail through rem sts and pull tightly to close tip, using tapestry needle. Sew side seam.
2. Attach A at cuff seam of one mitten, using crochet hook. Work a 6"-long ch and sl st at cuff seam of other mitten. Fasten off and weave in ends.

The Hunt

Featuring the main characters of the hunt—the horse and rider, the hounds, the horn, and of course, the fox—these quick-to-stitch pleasers will make fabulous gifts for the horse-and-hunt enthusiasts in your life.

DMC	Color
■ 310	black
· white	white
✳ 321	red
● 815	garnet, med.
○ 945	flesh
++ 922	copper, lt.
◑ 919	red-copper
◤ 300	mahogany, vy. dk.
/ 745	yellow, lt. pl.
⊗ 725	topaz
△ 648	beaver gray, lt.

△	680	old gold, dk.
	922	copper, lt.

v	919	red-copper
	922	copper, lt.

┌	300	mahogany, vy. dk.
	310	black

+	648	beaver gray, lt.
	white	white

Fabric: 28-count evergreen/dark teal linen from Wichelt Imports, Inc.

Stitch count:

Fox	24H x 27W
Horn	32H x 42W
Horse	39H x 40W
Hounds	25H x 38W

Design size:

Fox
25-count	2" x 2⅛"
28-count	1¾" x 2"
30-count	1⅝" x 1¾"
32-count	1½" x 1⅝"

Horn
25-count	2½" x 3⅜"
28-count	2¼" x 3"
30-count	2⅛" x 2¾"
32-count	2" x 2⅝"

Horse
25-count	3⅛" x 3¼"
28-count	2¾" x 2⅞"
30-count	2⅝" x 2⅝"
32-count	2½" x 2½"

Hounds
25-count	2" x 3"
28-count	1¾" x 2¾"
30-count	1⅝" x 2½"
32-count	1½" x 2⅜"

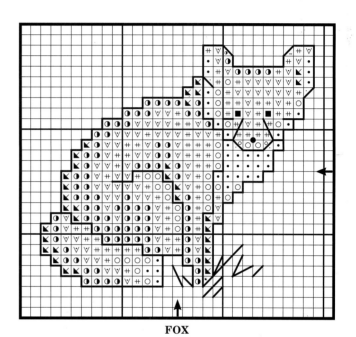

FOX

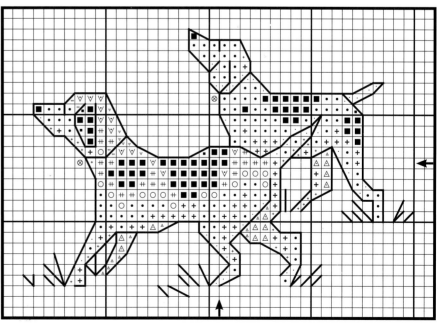

HOUNDS

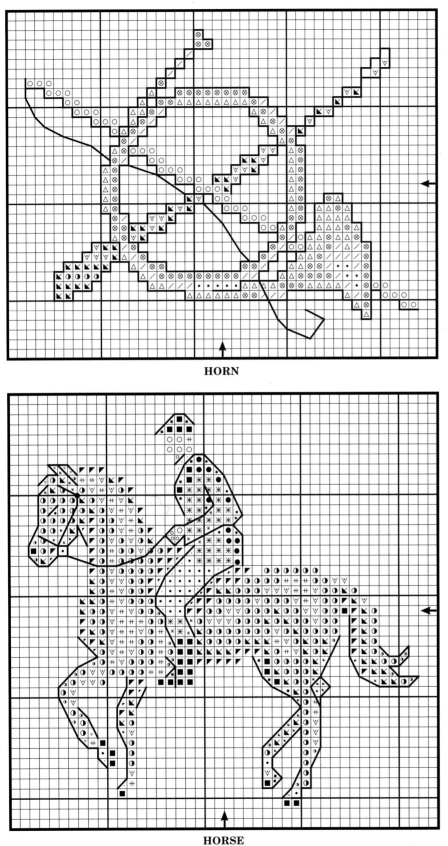

HORN

HORSE

Instructions: Cross stitch over two threads, using three strands of floss. Backstitch using one strand of floss unless otherwise indicated. Work French knots where • appears at intersecting grid lines, using two strands of floss and wrapping floss around needle once. Work straight stitches using one strand of floss. When two colors are bracketed together, use two strands of first color and one strand of second color.

Backstitch instructions:

Fox

300	all backstitching

Horn

922	whip (with rope)
310	riding crop
300	horn

Horse

922	hand, saddle iron
310	remainder of backstitching

Hounds

310	eyes
321	collars (two strands)
300	remainder of backstitching

French-knot instructions:

Fox

310	nose

Horse

white	bridle

Straight-stitch instructions:

Fox

922	grass

Horn

922	whip

Horse

310	reins, bridle

Hounds

922	grass

Finishing materials:

5½" square fabric for **each** ornament (for backing)

18" length white rattail cord for **each** ornament (for trim and hanger)

Finishing:

Turn to page **131** for "Basic Ornament-Finishing Instructions."

FRENCH KNOT

Holiday Animals

Pets are a part of the family, too, as any animal lover will tell you. We think these darling, stitched ornaments provide a whimsical way to give a gift of Christmas cheer to a friend and her furry, or feathered, companion! Fill a small basket with treats for Spot or Fluffy, and complete the presentation with a stitched ornament for the pet's owner.

Holiday Animals

DMC	Color
· white	white
⧻ 350	coral, med.
◑ 321	red
● 815	garnet, med.
◖ 3021	brown-gray, dk.
⊙ 318	steel gray, lt.
L 963	dusty rose, vy. lt.
⋎ 890	pistachio, ul. dk.
▵ 367	pistachio, dk.
9 368	pistachio, lt.
▲ 3776	mahogany, lt.
∽ 437	tan, lt.
╱ 739	tan, ul. lt.
⦉ 841	beige-brown, lt.
✗ 535	ash gray, vy. lt.
╲ 745	yellow, lt. pl.
♡ 725	topaz
◐ 435	brown, vy. lt.
⬈ ⌈ white	white
⌊ 318	steel gray, lt.
∷ ⌈ 739	tan, ul. lt.
⌊ 841	beige-brown, lt.
⊗ ⌈ 437	tan, lt.
⌊ 3776	mahogany, lt.
◕ ⌈ 318	steel gray, lt.
⌊ 535	ash gray, vy. lt.
⦅ ⌈ 745	yellow, lt. pl.
⌊ 725	topaz
✳ ⌈ 435	brown, vy. lt.
⌊ 725	topaz

Fabric: 28-count antique green linen from Wichelt Imports, Inc.

Stitch count:

Puppy	39H x 41W
Bird	42H x 22W
Kitten	36H x 20W
Bunnies	19H x 42W

Design size:

Puppy
16-count	2⅜" x 2½"
18-count	2⅛" x 2¼"
25-count	3⅛" x 3¼"
28-count	2¾" x 3"

Bird
16-count	2⅝" x 1⅜"
18-count	2⅜" x 1¼"
25-count	3⅜" x 1¾"
28-count	3" x 1½"

Kitten
16-count	2¼" x 1¼"
18-count	2" x 1⅛"
25-count	2⅞" x 1⅝"
28-count	2½" x 1½"

Bunnies
16-count	1⅛" x 2⅝"
18-count	1" x 2⅜"
25-count	1½" x 3⅜"
28-count	1⅜" x 3"

Instructions: Cross stitch over two threads, using three strands of floss. Backstitch using one strand of floss. Work French knots where ● appears at intersecting grid lines, using two strands of floss and wrapping floss around needle once. Make straight stitches using one strand of floss. When two colors are bracketed together, use two strands of first color and one strand of second color.

Backstitch instructions:

Puppy
3021	puppy, tassels
890	pillow

Bird
435	bird

3021	beak
890	perch
815	red ribbon

Kitten
815	ball of yarn
321	strand of yarn in paw
535	kitten
725	bottom of eyes
435	bells

Bunnies
3021	bunny with red ribbon
841	bunny with green ribbon
890	green bow
815	red bow

French-knot instructions:

Puppy
3021	eyes
white	nose

Bird
3021	eye

Straight-stitch instructions:

Puppy
3021	tassels

Kitten
321	strand of yarn from mouth to ball
white	whiskers

Bunnies
white	whiskers

Finishing materials:

6" square fabric for **each** ornament (for backing)

18" length red piping for **each** ornament

7" length red floss for **each** ornament (for hanger)

Finishing:

Turn to page **131** for "Basic Ornament-Finishing Instructions."

FRENCH KNOT

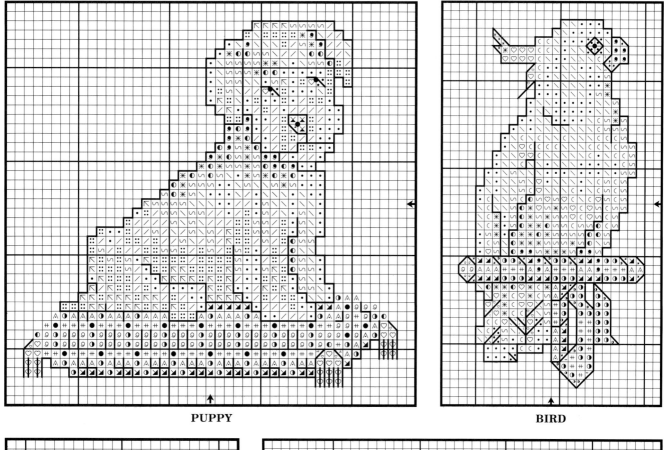

PUPPY

BIRD

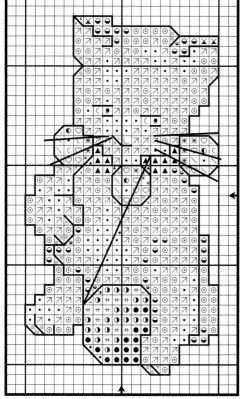

KITTEN

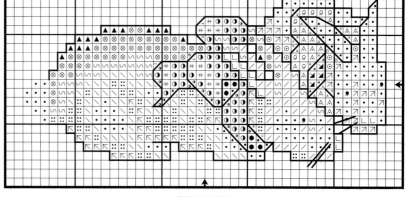

BUNNIES

51

Holiday Traditions

Trends may come and go, but classic Christmas is always in style. Because we know that traditional Christmas colors, styles, and motifs tend to be the most popular of all types for seasonal decorating, we have filled this chapter with ornaments inspired by the age-old traditions of this most joyous of all seasons. You'll find Smocked Flowers & Trees ornaments, a Nutcracker Beadwork collection, and several timeless cross-stitch designs. The ornaments that follow are certain to have you making your list, checking it twice, and humming all the while as you watch for that jolly character in red to make his annual appearance!

First Christmas

Life is filled with important "firsts," and Christmas is one of them! Mark your first holiday season together as a couple or celebrate a baby's first yuletide with these pleasing, first-Christmas ornaments. A single design is given for couples, and similar inspirations—one for a boy and one for a girl—are included for infants. An alphabet and numerals chart is included for personalization.

OUR FIRST CHRISTMAS

First Christmas

	Kreinik	
DMC	**Metallics**	**Color**
· white		white
○ 677		old gold, vy. lt.
H 436		tan
v 743		yellow, med.
+ 945		flesh
/ 955		nile green, lt.
⊗ 794		cornflower, lt.
♥ 666		red, bt.

∽ 892	carnation, med.
\ 519	sky blue
⊰ 807	peacock
✍ 3765	peacock, vy. dk.
к 311	navy, med.
⏀ 368	pistachio, lt.
● 367	pistachio, dk.
■ 319	pistachio, vy. dk.
⌐⌐[436 / 677	tan / old gold, vy. lt.
↑[436 / 002-BF	tan / gold

● 801 coffee, dk.
bs 5 Japan gold

Fabric: 28-count ruby red linen from Wichelt Imports, Inc.

Stitch count:

| *Our First Christmas* | 66H x 48W |
| *Baby's First Christmas* | 64H x 46W |

Design size:

Our First Christmas

| 25-count | 5¼" x 3⅞" |
| 28-count | 4¾" x 3½" |

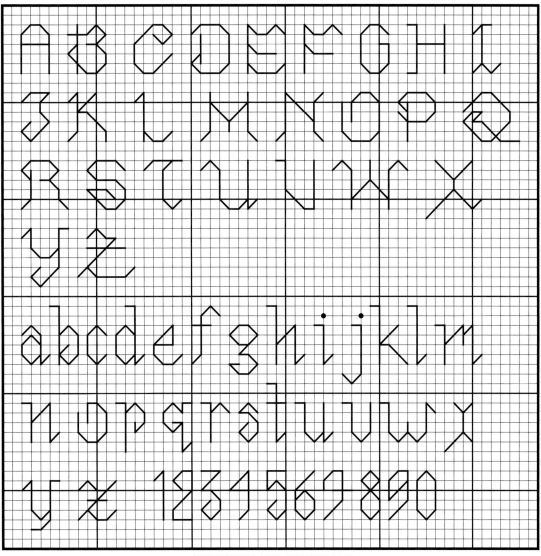

ALPHABET AND NUMERALS

32-count	4⅛" x 3"
36-count	3⅝" x 2⅝"

Baby's First Christmas

25-count	5⅛" x 3⅝"
28-count	4½" x 3¼"
32-count	4" x 2⅞"
36-count	3½" x 2½"

Instructions: Cross stitch over two threads, using three strands of floss unless otherwise indicated. Backstitch (bs) using one strand of floss. Work French knots using two strands of floss and wrapping floss around needle once. Work straight stitch using two strands of floss or one strand Kreinik #5 Japan Gold. When two colors are bracketed together, use two strands of first color and one strand of second color. When blending floss and Kreinik Metallics, use two strands of floss and two strands Kreinik blending filament.

Backstitch (bs) instructions:
677	lettering
801	rocking horse, bell, faces, hands, gold ribbon, birds, windowsill
319	clothing
743	yellow ribbon
666	red ribbon, curtain edge (two strands)
436	outer edge of candle flames
#5	curtain design

Straight-stitch instructions:
white	outer edge of star, inside of candle flames
#5	lines radiating from star

French-knot instructions:
677	dot of letter *i*
743	bell

Finishing:
Turn to page **131** for "Basic Ornament-Finishing Instructions." Turn to page **141** for "How-Tos for Making Twisted Cording."

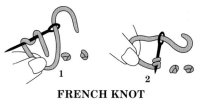

FRENCH KNOT

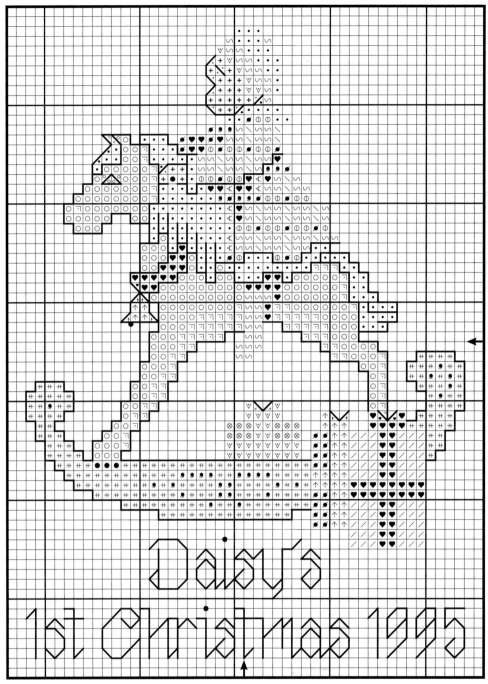

BABY'S FIRST CHRISTMAS (GIRL)

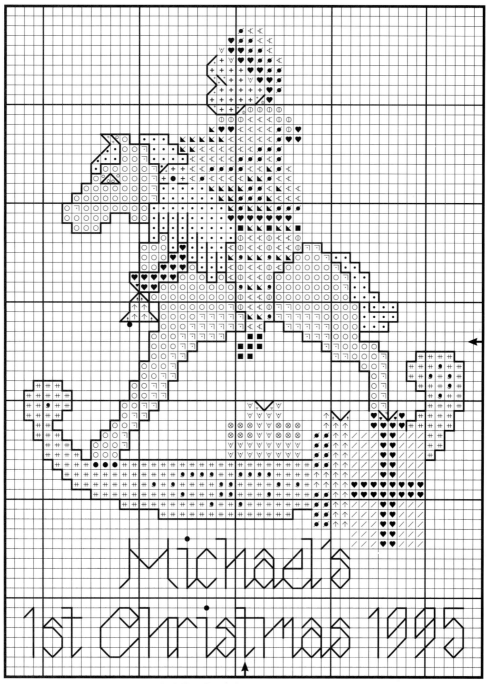

BABY'S FIRST CHRISTMAS (BOY)

Candy-Cane Christmas

A red-and-white border that resembles a candy cane surrounds each of these adorable branch trimmers. Including a darling teddy bear, a colorful train engine, a tricycle, a toy horse, and a jolly Santa, these designs are certain to bring smiles to all who see them. These little ornaments look fantastic on the tree, but will also make great package tags for children of all ages!

DMC	Color
· white	white
∕ 746	off white
— 3347	yellow-green, med.
M 3346	hunter
✕ 3345	hunter, dk.
■ 895	green, dk.
∨ 725	topaz
☉ 783	gold
L 3712	salmon, med.
⋏ 3328	salmon, med.
◑ 347	salmon, dk.
▲ 498	red, dk.
✳ 310	black
T 422	hazelnut, lt.
↙ 420	hazelnut, dk.
·∣·[422	hazelnut, lt.
420	hazelnut, dk.
X 760	salmon

•	413	pewter gray, dk.
‖	762	pearl gray, vy. lt.
∽	415	pearl gray
+ ⎡	white	white
⎣	775	baby blue, lt.
○	775	baby blue, lt.
=	948	peach flesh, vy. lt.
ℓ	822	beige-gray, lt.
ɢ	838	beige-brown, vy. dk.
⅍ ⎡	760	salmon
⎣	948	peach flesh, vy. lt.

Fabric: 32-count teal green Belfast linen from Zweigart®
Stitch count: 48H x 48W
Design size:

14-count	3⅜" x 3⅜"
18-count	2⅝" x 2⅝"
28-count	3⅜" x 3⅜"

32-count   3" x 3"

Instructions: Cross stitch over two threads, using two strands of floss. Backstitch using one strand of floss. Work French knots where • appears at intersecting grid lines, using two strands of floss and wrapping floss around needle once unless otherwise indicated. Make straight stitches using one strand of floss. Work lazy-daisy stitch where symbol ○ appears, using two strands 3712. When two colors are bracketed together, use one strand of each.

Backstitch instructions:
Horse

| 310 | tail, eyelashes |
| 838 | remainder of backstitching |

Teddy Bear

| 838 | all backstitching |

Tricycle

762	wheels, seat, handles, boots
347	red parts of tricycle
775	white and light-blue parts of tricycle
725	headlight
3712	doll's mouth
838	remainder of backstitching

Train

3347	green parts of train
762	black parts of train
498	red parts of train
420	inner and outer edges of wheels, bell, bell stand, gold parts of train
white	bubbles
895	leaf on train

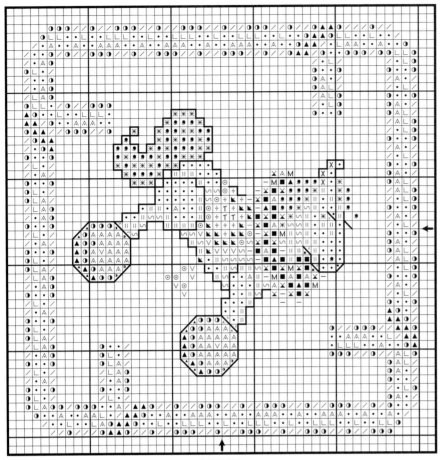

HORSE

Santa
895 holly leaves
413 fur on hat, beard
838 eyes, nose, lower lip

French-knot instructions:
Tricycle
838 doll's eyes
760 doll's cheeks
725 buttons on doll's dress
3712 knots in hair bows
Train
white bubbles, string in cab (wrap twice)
725 bell
347 berries, wheel spokes
Santa
498 holly berries

Straight-stitch instructions:
Tricycle
762 tire spokes
3712 bow streamers
Train
347 N
725 O, wheel spokes
895 E
775 L
white string in cab

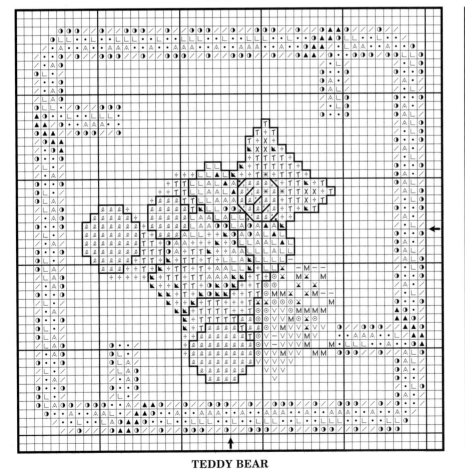

TEDDY BEAR

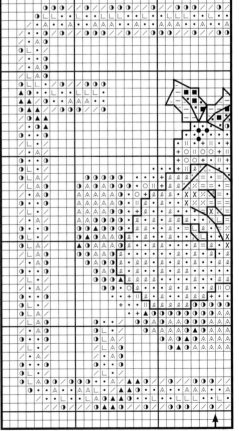

SANTA

Finishing materials:
4" square fabric for **each** ornament
  (for backing)
20" length twisted cording for **each**
  ornament (for trim and hanger)

Finishing:
Turn to page **131** for "Basic Ornament-Finishing Instructions." Turn to page **141** for "How-tos for Making Twisted Cording."

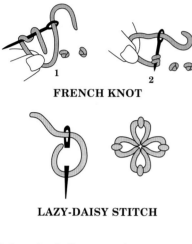

FRENCH KNOT

LAZY-DAISY STITCH

Shaded portion indicates overlap from previous page.

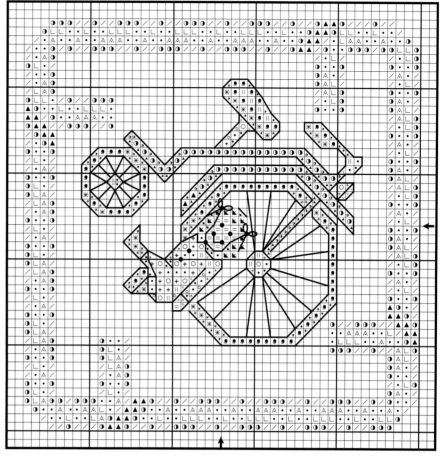

TRICYCLE

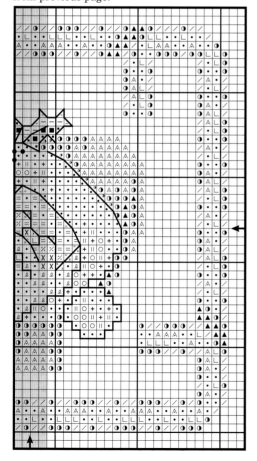

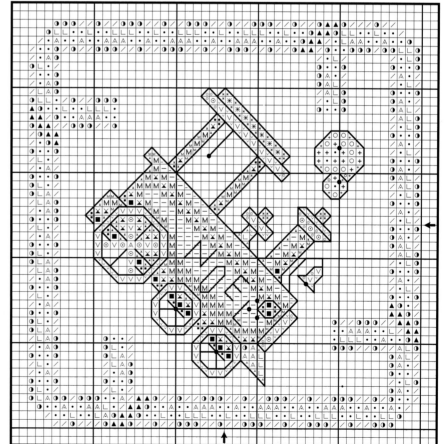

TRAIN

The First Christmas

The story of the first Christmas is told in stitches in this set of seven, uniquely shaped ornaments. Worked in cross stitch using cotton floss and blending filament, each piece is finished as a lightly stuffed ornament and trimmed with decorative beads, twisted-floss hangers, and complementary tassels. The shapes of these tree trimmers, inspired by the elongated, glass ornaments that have made a comeback in popularity over the last few holiday seasons, make them a challenge to finish; but we think you will be absolutely thrilled with the results of your efforts!

	DMC	Kreinik Balger®	Color
●	730		olive, vy. dk.
■	310		black
⊂	340		blue violet, med.
H	553		violet, med.
⌐	778		mauve, lt.
▬	676		old gold, lt.
◗	995		electric blue, dk.
\	3072		beaver gray, vy. lt.
8	826		blue, med.
/	3325		baby blue
○	3779		terra cotta, ul. vy. lt.
▲	3781		mocha brown, dk.
△	3782		mocha brown, lt.
3	833		olive, lt.
◑	600		cranberry, vy. dk.
◤	917		plum, med.
X	523		fern green, lt.
◥	3346		hunter
ıᒉ	3072		beaver gray, vy. lt.
		001HL	silver
ℓᒉ	699		green
		009HL	emerald
Sᒉ	666		red, bt.
		003HL	red
♥ᒉ	995		electric blue, dk.
		006	blue
αᒉ	676		old gold, lt.
		002	gold

Fabrics: 11-count Victorian Christmas red Pearl Aida from Zweigart®, 22-count beige Hardanger from Zweigart®, 22-count Christmas green Hardanger from Wichelt Imports, Inc., 22-count dark-blue Hardanger from Wichelt Imports, Inc.

Stitch count:

Shepherd & Lamb	50H x 20W
Balthazar, Melchoir, Herald Angel	39H x 29W
Kaspar, Holy Family, Madonna & Child	46H x 20W

Design size:

Shepherd & Lamb

11-count	4½" x 1⅞"
14-count	3½" x 1⅜"
18-count	2¾" x 1⅛"
22-count	4½" x 1⅞"

Balthazar, Melchoir, Herald Angel

11-count	3½" x 2⅝"
14-count	2¾" x 2"
18-count	2⅛" x 1⅝"
22-count	3½" x 2⅝"

Kaspar, Holy Family, Madonna & Child

11-count	4⅛" x 1⅞"
14-count	3¼" x 1⅜"
18-count	2½" x 1⅛"
22-count	4⅛" x 1⅞"

Instructions: Cross stitch using four strands of floss when stitching on Aida. Cross stitch over two threads, using four strands of floss, when stitching on Hardanger. Backstitch using one strand of floss unless otherwise indicated. Work French knots where ● appears at intersecting grid lines, using two strands of floss and wrapping floss around needle once. When two colors are bracketed together, use two strands of each.

Backstitch instructions:

Shepherd & Lamb

676	inner and outer edges of ornament border
3781	shepherd's staff (two strands)
001HL	star
310	sheep's legs (two strands)
310	remainder of backstitching

Balthazar

676	inner and outer edges of ornament border
001HL	star
310	remainder of backstitching

Melchoir

699	inner and outer edges of ornament border
310	remainder of backstitching

Herald Angel

995	inner and outer edges of ornament border
676	rays from halo (two strands)
310	remainder of backstitching

Kaspar

666	inner and outer edges of ornament border
001HL	star
310	remainder of backstitching

Holy Family

666	inner and outer edges of ornament border
001HL	star
310	remainder of backstitching

Madonna & Child

699	inner and outer edges of ornament border
310	remainder of backstitching

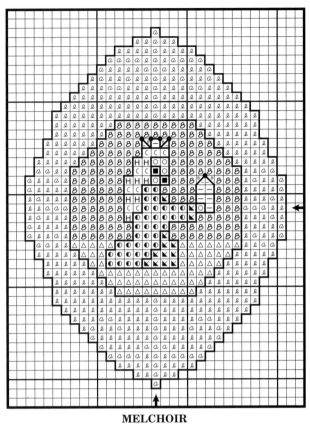

MELCHOIR

1   2

FRENCH KNOT

French-knot instructions:

Shepherd & Lamb
310   Shepherd's eye
Balthazar
676   crown
310   camel's eye
Melchoir
676   crown, gift
Kaspar
310   eye

Finishing materials:
6" square fabric for **each** ornament (for backing)
10" length twisted-cord hanger for **each** ornament
1 tassel for **each** ornament
2 decorative beads for **each** ornament

Finishing:
Turn to page **131** for "Basic Ornament-Finishing Instructions." Turn to page **141** for "How-Tos for Making Twisted Cording." Turn to page **101** for tassel-making instructions, and use a 3" card.

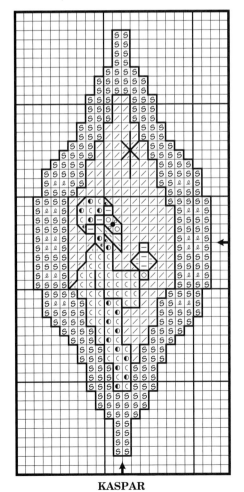

KASPAR

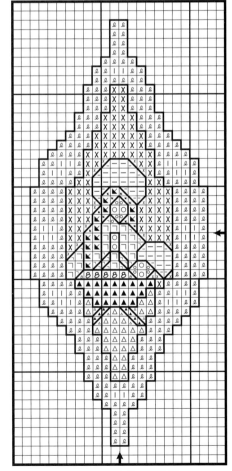

MADONNA & CHILD

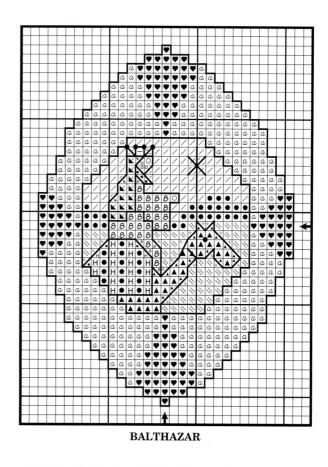

HERALD ANGEL

BALTHAZAR

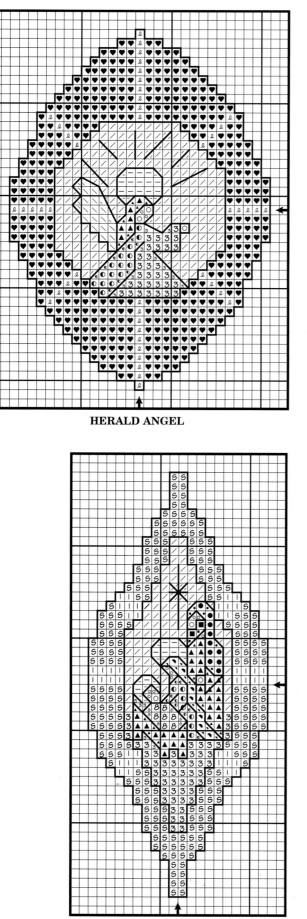

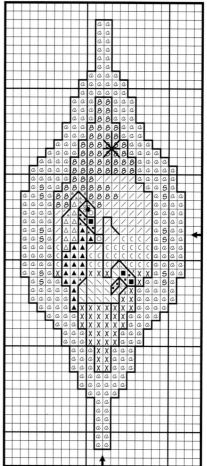

HOLY FAMILY

SHEPHERD & LAMB

Nutcracker Beadwork

The principal characters of The Nutcracker Suite *ballet are portrayed in cross stitch and beadwork in this charming set of ornaments. Worked on perforated paper, each figure is then cut out around the perimeter of the stitching and beading to accentuate its interesting shape. If your little girl is dancing in this annual ballet, or if you know a little girl who is, why not make this collection for her? These pieces would be positively delightful in her room, and would send her to bed each night with visions of sugarplums, or perhaps sugarplum fairies, dancing in her head!*

	DMC	DMC FT	Color
X		2415	pearl gray
ĸ		2414	steel gray, dk.
3	333		blue violet, dk.
•.	340		blue violet, med.
♥	791		cornflower, vy. dk.
\	776		pink, med.
●	310		black
6	321		red
ı	3774		peach flesh, vy. lt.
•	white		white
8	780		topaz, vy. dk.
●	3607		plum, lt.
—	800		delft, pl.
ᴗ	799		delft, med.
▲	413		pewter gray, dk.
⊖	415		pearl gray
⌐776			pink, med.
// 340			blue violet, med.
⌐3607			plum, lt.

Mill Hill Seed Beads

C	02011	Victorian gold
H	00423	tangerine
■	02014	black
⌐	00209	ice lilac
◑	00332	emerald
▽	00148	pale peach
+	00479	white
⍺	02013	red, red

Fabric: 14-count shiny gold perforated paper from Craft World® International, Inc.

Stitch count:

Nutcracker	64H x 50W
Mouse King	57H x 55W

Drosselmeyer	62H x 57W
Sugarplum Fairy	54H x 36W
Clara	63H x 26W

Design Size:

Nutcracker

14-count	4½" x 3½"
16-count	4" x 3⅛"
18-count	3½" x 2¾"
22-count	2⅞" x 2¼"

Mouse King

14-count	4⅛" x 4"
16-count	3½" x 3½"
18-count	3⅛" x 3"
22-count	2½" x 2½"

Drosselmeyer

14-count	4⅜" x 4⅛"
16-count	3⅞" x 3½"
18-count	3½" x 3⅛"
22-count	2⅞" x 2½"

Sugarplum Fairy

14-count	3⅞" x 2½"
16-count	3⅜" x 2¼"
18-count	3" x 2"
22-count	2½" x 1⅝"

Clara

14-count	4½" x 1⅞"
16-count	4" x 1⅝"
18-count	3½" x 1½"
22-count	2⅞" x 1⅛"

Instructions: Cross stitch using three strands of floss or two strands of DMC Flower Thread (DMC FT). Backstitch using one strand of floss. Make straight stitches on wings of *Sugarplum Fairy*, using one strand white. When three colors are bracketed together, use one strand of each.

Backstitch instructions:

310 Nutcracker's teeth, Drossel-
        meyer's eye
799 laces on Clara's slippers
321 Clara's mouth, Drosselmeyer's
        mouth, Sugarplum Fairy's
        slipper laces and mouth
776 Clara's nose
780 Sugarplum Fairy's eye

Finishing instructions:
Materials:

8" length metallic-gold thread for
each ornament (for hanger)
Small, sharp scissors
Beading needle

1. Complete stitching following instructions given.
2. Trim perforated paper around perimeter of stitching, leaving a paper
rim around perimeter.
3. Thread needle, insert through center top of ornament, and remove
needle. Tie thread ends in a knot to
form hanger.

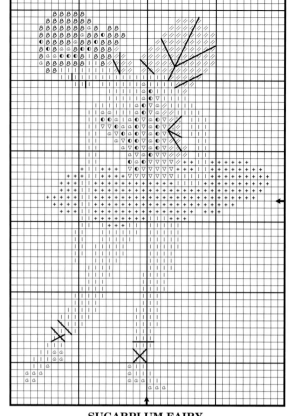

SUGARPLUM FAIRY

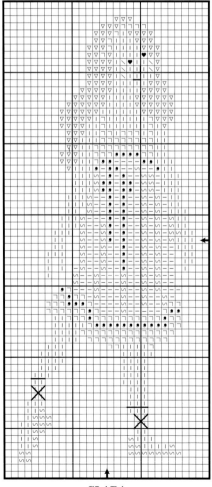

CLARA

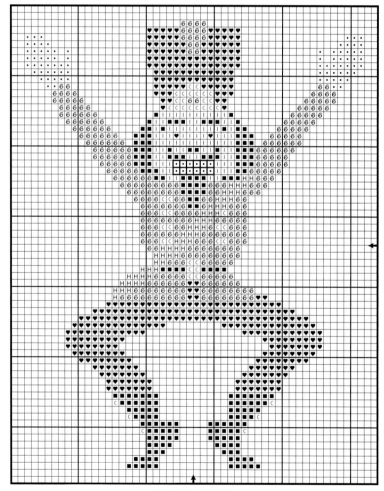

NUTCRACKER

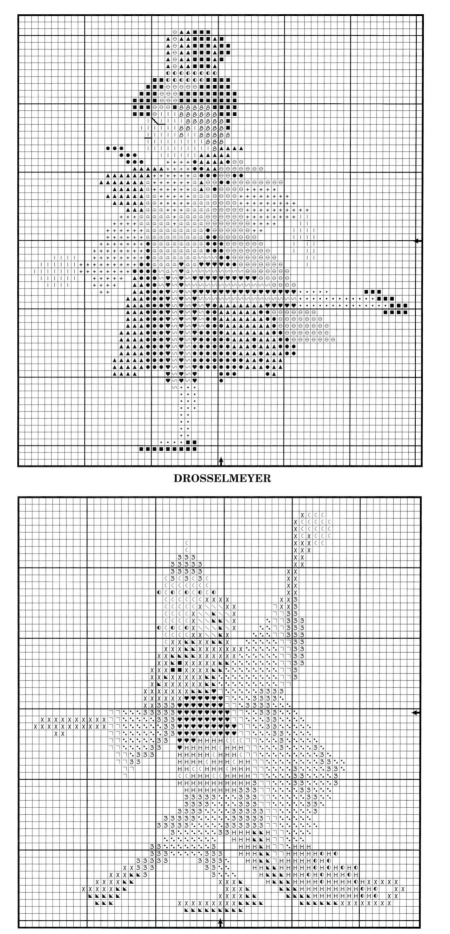

DROSSELMEYER

MOUSE KING

Smocked Flowers & Trees

Smocking, created using traditional colors, will add a distinctively different touch to your seasonal decorating. Whether used as ornaments displayed on the branches of your evergreen, or hung from furniture handles or lighting fixtures, these pieces will send a message of holiday cheer.

Materials:
¼" yd. **each** 44"-wide cotton fabric, colors: green, white
DMC embroidery floss, colors: #321 red, #909 green, white
Kreinik fine #8 braid, color: #002 gold
Mill Hill seed beads, colors: #00557 gold, #02013 red
3½" foam ball (for **each** ornament)
2 yds. ⅝"-wide metallic-gold ribbon (for *Smocked Flowers* ornament)
3 yds. ¼"-wide red satin ribbon (for *Smocked Trees* ornament)
Straight pins with flat metal heads
4 quilter's straight pins (with plastic heads)
Glue
Hand-sewing needle
Scissors

Smocked Flowers
1. Pleat fabric or have fabric pleated with eleven pleating threads. Design is worked on seven rows; leave two rows at top and bottom unworked for finishing. Block pleated panel to 10".
2. Work smocking using three strands floss or one strand fine braid. First and last three pleats will not be stitched.

Row 1: Beginning with an up cable, work across in cable stitch, using three strands 321.
Row 2: Beginning with a down cable, work across in cable stitch, using one strand 002.
Row 6: Beginning with an up cable, work across in cable stitch, using one strand 002.
Row 7: Beginning with a down cable, work across in cable stitch, using three strands 321.
Rows 2½–4: Beginning with a down cable on row 4, work a 1½-space, 5-step trellis—11 cable combination using three strands 321.

72

SMOCKED TREES ORNAMENT

SMOCKED FLOWERS ORNAMENT

Rows 4–5½: Beginning with an up cable on row 4, work a 1½-space, 5-step trellis–11 cable combination using three strands 321.

3. Work lazy-daisy-stitch flowers in center of each hexagon, using three strands white. Sew three gold seed beads in center of each flower.

4. Working in cable stitch, backsmock along wrong side of Rows 3, 4, and 5, using two strands 909.

Smocked Trees

1. Pleat fabric or have fabric pleated with thirteen pleating threads. Design is worked on nine rows; leave two rows at top and bottom unworked for finishing. Block pleated panel to 10".
2. Work smocking using three strands floss or one strand fine braid. First and last three pleats will not be stitched.

Rows 1 & 8: Beginning with an up cable, work across in cable stitch, using one strand 002.
Rows 2 & 9: Beginning with a down cable, work across in cable stitch, using one strand 002.
Rows 3, 4, 6, & 7: Beginning with a down cable, work across in cable stitch, using three strands 909.

Rows 2–2½: Beginning on row 2½, work ½-space wave stitches between rows 2 and 2½, using three strands 321.

Rows 7½–8: Beginning on row 7½, work ½-space wave stitch between rows 7½ and 8, using three strands 321.

3. Work trees individually in a 1½-space, 6-step trellis stitch, using three strands 909 and referring to chart for placement. Work tree topper by working individual cable stitch above green cable stitch at tree top, using one strand 002.

4. Work cable stitches as shown on chart on rows 3½ and 6½, using three strands 909.

5. Sew red seed beads where symbol ● appears on chart.

6. Working in cable stitch on wrong side of panel, backsmock along row 5, using two strands white.

Finishing instructions:

1. Remove pleating threads from rows containing stitching. Trim fabric above and below top and bottom pleating threads to ¼"; press to wrong side. Wrap smocked panel around foam ball; turn back unsmocked seam allowance on one side and lap it over the other side. Pin through all layers into foam ball, aligning rows of smocking. Pull gently on second and tenth pleating threads for flower ornament, and second and twelfth pleating threads for tree ornament, to gather around top and bottom of ball. Tie pleating threads together; align and pin these rows in place. Tighten and secure top and bottom pleating threads in same manner, having ¼" allowances tucked inside. Pin gathered pleats in place at top and bottom of ball, pinning until smooth.

2. For each ornament, cut 7" length from ribbon for hanger. Form a loop and pin through ends with quilter's pin. Cut remaining ribbon into two, equal pieces. To make a multi-loop bow, pin through end of one length of ribbon, estimate a 3" length and pierce ribbon again, forming a loop. Continue making loops with remainder of ribbon. Loops will spread into flowerette as you work; arrange as desired. Use second length of ribbon to make a second, multi-loop bow without hanger for bottom of ornament. Place a dot of glue in top center and bottom openings and on pins. Pin bows to top and bottom of ornament, and let glue dry.

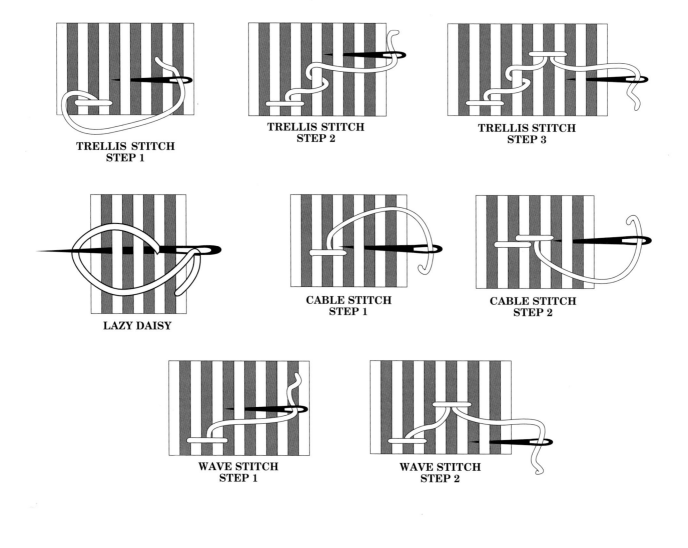

TRELLIS STITCH
STEP 1

TRELLIS STITCH
STEP 2

TRELLIS STITCH
STEP 3

LAZY DAISY

CABLE STITCH
STEP 1

CABLE STITCH
STEP 2

WAVE STITCH
STEP 1

WAVE STITCH
STEP 2

Holiday Trio

Perforated paper makes unique finishing possible with this set of holiday-inspired ornaments. Each design has two parts, each of which is worked on a separate piece of perforated paper. The paper is then trimmed close to the edge of each stitched design, and the pieces are assembled to create a dimensional effect. Choose your favorite from the angel, the sleigh, or Santa—or stitch all three and display them on an indoor wreath, as shown here.

Holiday Trio

DMC	Color
· white	white
○ 304	red, med.
U 319	pistachio, vy. dk.
▲ 320	pistachio, med.
Z 353	peach flesh
♡ 422	hazelnut, lt.
S 501	blue green, dk.
△ 503	blue green, med.
C 504	blue green, lt.
− 676	old gold, lt.
╱ 677	old gold, vy. lt.
ℓ 725	topaz
⫽ 739	tan, ul. lt.
‥ 746	off white
ı 754	peach flesh, lt.
+ 762	pearl gray, vy. lt.
◆ 781	topaz, dk.
X 798	delft, dk.
✳ 816	garnet
bs 500	blue green, vy. dk.
bs 3799	pewter gray, dk.

Kreinik Fine (#8) Braid

L 002HL	gold
● 085	peacock

Fabric: 14-count ivory perforated paper from Yarn Tree Designs

Stitch count:

Angel	40H x 37W
Wings	20H x 34W
Kriss Kringle	42H x 29W
Bag of Toys	23H x 20W
Sleigh	23H x 41W
Gifts in Sleigh	21H x 34W

Design size:

Angel	
14-count	2⅞" x 2⅝"
16-count	2½" x 2⅜"
18-count	2¼" x 2"
22-count	1⅞" x 1¾"
Wings	
14-count	1⅜" x 2½"
16-count	1¼" x 2⅛"
18-count	1⅛" x 1⅞"
22-count	1" x 1½"
Kriss Kringle	
14-count	3" x 2"
16-count	2⅝" x 1⅞"
18-count	2⅜" x 1⅝"
22-count	2" x 1⅜"
Bag of Toys	
14-count	1⅝" x 1⅜"
16-count	1½" x 1¼"
18-count	1¼" x 1⅛"
22-count	1" x 1"
Sleigh	
14-count	1⅝" x 3"
16-count	1½" x 2½"
18-count	1¼" x 2¼"
22-count	1" x 1⅞"
Gifts in Sleigh	
14-count	1½" x 2½"
16-count	1⅜" x 2⅛"
18-count	1⅛" x 1⅞"
22-count	1" x 1½"

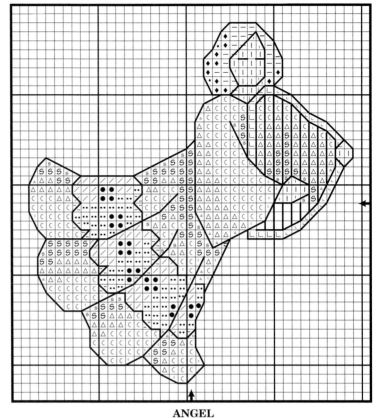

ANGEL

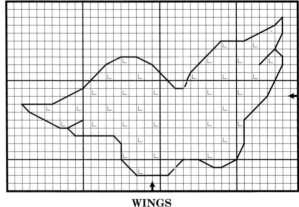

WINGS

Instructions: Cross stitch using three strands of floss or one strand of braid. Backstitch (bs) using two strands of floss or one strand of braid. Work French knots for doll's eyes, using one strand 798 and wrapping floss around needle three times.

Backstitch (bs) instructions:

Angel
002HL	robe trim, harp strings
500	remainder of backstitching

Wings
085	outline of wings

Kriss Kringle
002HL	cuff stripes, coat-front trim
3799	remainder of backstitching

Bag of Toys
002HL	stripes on white block of bag
319	tension cords on drum
304	doll's mouth
3799	remainder of backstitching

Sleigh
816	design in corner of sleigh
3799	remainder of backstitching

Gifts in Sleigh
002HL	stripes on white gift on far right
304	stripes on white gift in center, ribbon on blue gift in center
3799	remainder of backstitching

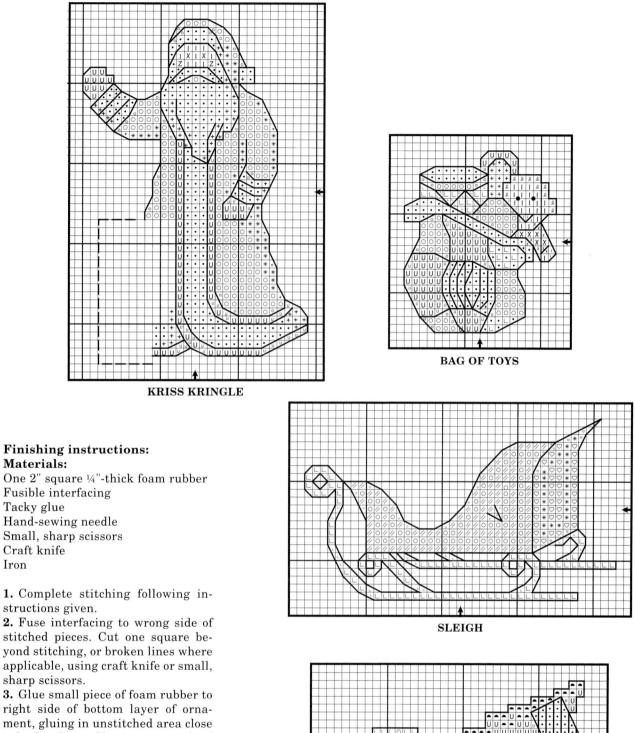

KRISS KRINGLE

BAG OF TOYS

SLEIGH

GIFTS IN SLEIGH

Finishing instructions:
Materials:
One 2" square ¼"-thick foam rubber
Fusible interfacing
Tacky glue
Hand-sewing needle
Small, sharp scissors
Craft knife
Iron

1. Complete stitching following instructions given.
2. Fuse interfacing to wrong side of stitched pieces. Cut one square beyond stitching, or broken lines where applicable, using craft knife or small, sharp scissors.
3. Glue small piece of foam rubber to right side of bottom layer of ornament, gluing in unstitched area close to broken lines. Glue to wrong side of top layer of ornament.
4. Thread needle with 7" length of gold braid, stitch through center top of ornament, and tie a knot in braid ends to form hanger.

FRENCH KNOT

77

A Very Victorian Yule

If your idea of the best holiday decorations includes those pieces that possess a touch of breathtaking, Victorian-inspired design, then the offerings on the following pages will be positively perfect for you. You'll find Counterchange Smocked Ornaments, *made using pretty, pastel shades; petit point* Feathered Friends, *worked on silk gauze; and boldly colored* Tassel Treasures. *Crazy quilting, silk-ribbon embroidery, and patchwork are all here to inspire you to make this Christmas your most memorable ever.*

Victorian Silk-Ribbon Treasures

Stretch your decorating possibilities to include multiple seasons with this quintet of engaging ornaments! Perfect for use on a Victorian-inspired Christmas tree, these designs can also make an appearance during Easter and throughout springtime to add a whimsical, inviting touch wherever they're displayed.

YLI Silk Ribbon (4mm)
☐	8	pink, lt.
☐	18	green, lt.
▨	19	green, med.
■	61	green, dk.
■	82	blue, dk.
▨	102	lavender
▨	152	pink, med.
▨	153	pink, dk.

DMC	**Color**
826	blue, med.
841	beige-brown, lt.
912	emerald, lt.
3746	blue violet, dk.
3755	baby blue

Mill Hill Pebble Beads
05168   sapphire

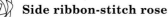

⬡	**Coral-Stitch rose**
⬖	**Rosette buds**
◊	**Japanese ribbon stitch**
✤	**Ribbon-Stitch rose**
◉	**Side ribbon-stitch rose**
○	**Montano knot**
⬭⬭⬭	**Chain stitch**
╲	**Backstitch**
❧	**Lazy-daisy stitch**

Note: For these projects, a general materials list has been given. Specific materials for each project have been listed separately.

General materials:
Assorted print fabrics, colors: yellow, light blue, dark blue, green, tan, pink
Small piece lavender solid fabric
Tacky glue
Tracing paper
Pencil
Hand-sewing needle with large eye
Scissors

Heart
Materials:
7" square pink-print fabric
4" x 5" piece white felt (for backing)
4" x 5" piece cardboard

1. Trace pattern onto fabric and work design.
2. Trace around perimeter of pattern on white felt and cardboard and cut out.
3. Trim stitched front to within ⅜" of perimeter of pattern. Center atop cardboard, turn raw edges to back side of cardboard, and glue in place. Let dry.
Note: Trimming seam allowances and clipping curves may be necessary for a smooth fit when turning raw edges to back side of cardboard.
4. Cut complementary ribbon to length of your choice for hanger. Bring ribbon ends together to form hanging loop, and glue in place on back side of ornament at top center. Glue felt to back side of ornament, being careful to align edge of felt with edge of cardboard around perimeter of ornament. Let dry.

Fan
Materials:
8" x 6½" piece green-print fabric
4" x 5" piece white felt (for backing)
4" x 5" piece cardboard

1. Trace pattern onto fabric and work design. Backstitch using two strands DMC 912.
2. Finish as for *Heart* ornament.

Basket
Materials:
7" square tan-print fabric
4" x 5" piece white felt (for backing)
4" x 5" piece cardboard

1. Trace pattern onto fabric and work design. Backstitch using two strands DMC 841. Work chain stitch using two strands DMC 841.
2. Finish as for *Heart* ornament.

Shoe
Materials:
6" square blue-print fabric
6" x 3" piece lavender fabric
4" x 5" piece white felt (for backing)
4" x 5" piece cardboard

1. Trace pattern onto fabric and work design. Appliqué toe piece to shoe. Work chain stitch at edge of toe piece, using three strands DMC 3746. Work satin stitch for heel, using two strands DMC 826 for inner edge and two strands DMC 3755 for outer edge. Glue pebble beads along edge of shoe, referring to photo for placement.
2. Finish as for *Heart* ornament.

Teapot
Materials:
8" x 7" piece yellow-print fabric
4" x 3" piece blue-print fabric
4" x 6" piece white felt (for backing)
4" x 6" piece cardboard

1. Trace pattern onto fabric. Appliqué heart to teapot. Work design.
2. Finish as for *Heart* ornament.

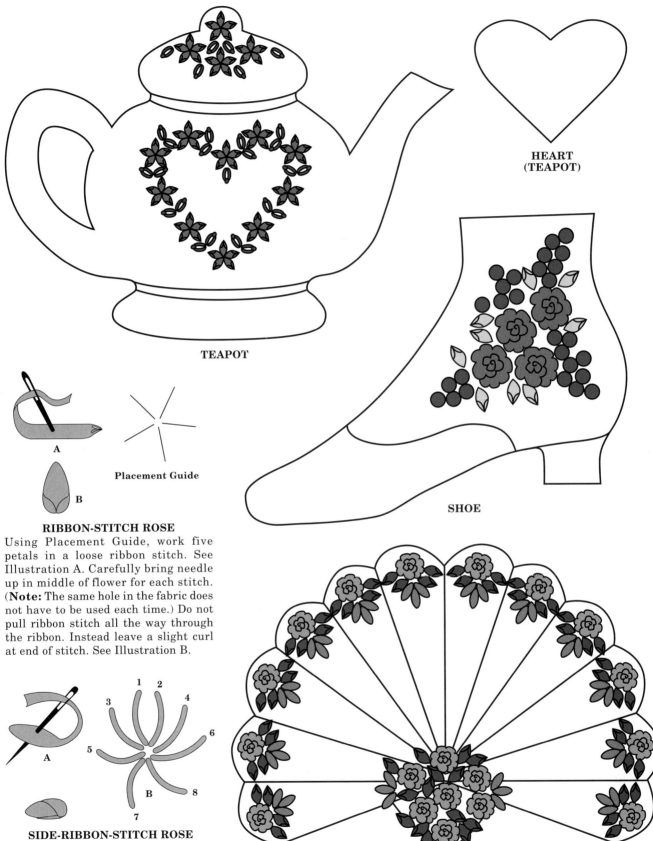

TEAPOT

HEART (TEAPOT)

SHOE

FAN

Placement Guide

RIBBON-STITCH ROSE
Using Placement Guide, work five petals in a loose ribbon stitch. See Illustration A. Carefully bring needle up in middle of flower for each stitch. (**Note:** The same hole in the fabric does not have to be used each time.) Do not pull ribbon stitch all the way through the ribbon. Instead leave a slight curl at end of stitch. See Illustration B.

SIDE-RIBBON-STITCH ROSE
Work petals in a loose side ribbon stitch. See Illustration A. Place petals according to numbers, taking needle down at each number. See Illustration B.

82

MONTANO KNOT

Bring needle up from back and circle ribbon around needle (six, five, four, three, two, or one time). Hold ribbon very loosely. (**Note:** Do not hold ribbon off to one side.) Insert needle back into fabric, as close to starting point as possible. Do not pull tight; let knot remain loose and flowery.

BASKET

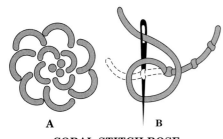

A   B

CORAL-STITCH ROSE

Work three French knots close together in a triangle shape to form center. See Illustration A. Work petals in a loose coral stitch, working in a clockwise direction. See Illustration B. Work four stitches in inner round, and seven in outer round.
Note: The number of stitches you use will depend on your tension, and on length of each stitch.

ROSETTE BUD

Make a padded straight stitch. Bring needle up at A. Insert needle at B, making a small straight stitch and keeping ribbon flat. Bring needle up at C and go down at D, creating a second straight stitch.

HEART

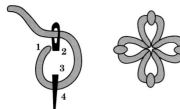

LAZY-DAISY STITCH

CHAIN STITCH

SATIN STITCH

JAPANESE RIBBON STITCH

Feathered Friends

Unique finishing makes these birds of a feather flock together for the holiday season. Shown as diminutive framed pieces with mirrors as backgrounds, these tiny designs will be lovely when hung from the branches of a sturdy evergreen. They have the added benefit of being ideal for year-round use; simply display them together on a favorite wall.

Kreinik
Soie

	Perlee	DMC	Color
◗	935	349	coral, dk.
∟	932	352	coral, lt.
■	noir	310	black
✳	114	995	electric blue, dk.
╱	113	996	electric blue, med.
◗	225	699	green
‡	224	701	green, lt.
•	221	704	chartreuse, bt.
+	2522	727	topaz, vy. lt.
◑	1734	647	beaver gray, med.
╲	blanc	white	white
∙∙	1712	3753	antique blue, ul. vy. lt.
⊾	161	823	navy, dk.
△	531	746	off white
⊅	4124	938	coffee, ul. dk.
◖	4122	433	brown, med.
⊙	633	721	spice, med.
↑	631	402	mahogany, vy. lt.

Fabric: 30-count Polysil™ gauze from Kreinik Manufacturing Company, Inc.

Stitch count:

Bird 1	27H x 52W
Bird 2	32H x 51W
Bird 3	32H x 45W
Bird 4	30H x 50W
Bird 5	32H x 46W

Design size:
Bird 1

25-count	2⅛" x 4⅛"
28-count	2" x 3¾"
30-count	1" x 1¾"
36-count	1½" x 2⅞"

Bird 2

25-count	2½" x 4"
28-count	2¼" x 3⅝"
30-count	1" x 1¾"
36-count	1¾" x 2⅞"

Bird 3

25-count	2½" x 3⅝"
28-count	2¼" x 3¼"
30-count	1" x 1½"
36-count	1¾" x 2½"

Bird 4

25-count	2½" x 4"
28-count	2⅛" x 3½"
30-count	1" x 1⅝"
36-count	1⅝" x 2¾"

Bird 5

25-count	2½" x 3⅝"
28-count	2¼" x 3¼"
30-count	1" x 1½"
36-count	1¾" x 2½"

Instructions: Work petit point using one strand of silk.

Note: *Bird 1* was also cross stitched over two threads on 36-count white Edinborough linen from Zweigart®, using two strands Kreinik Soie d'Alger.

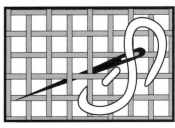

PETIT POINT

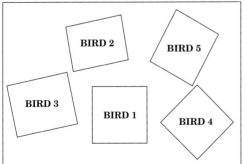

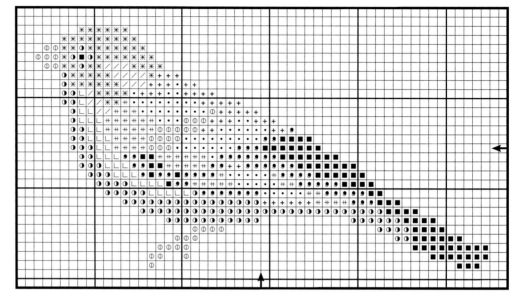

BIRD 1

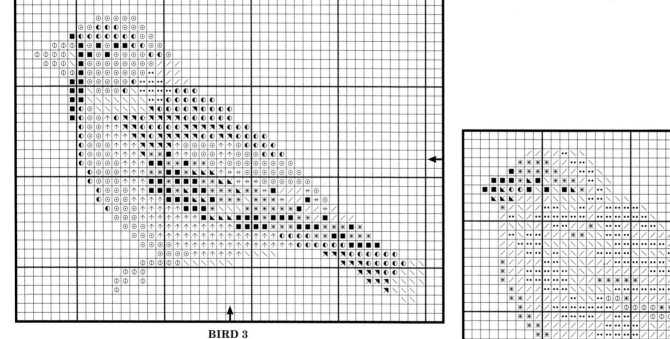

BIRD 3

BIRD 4

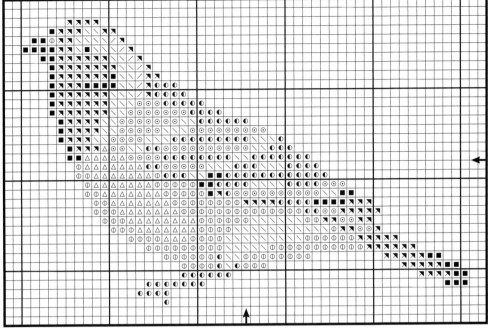

BIRD 2

Shaded portion indicates
overlap from previous page.

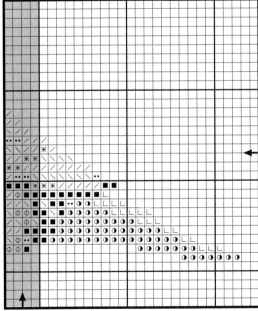

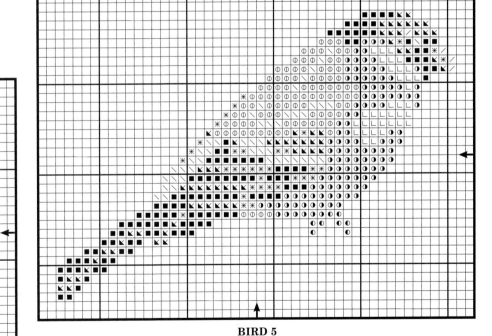

BIRD 5

Crazy-Quilt Ornaments

If the thought of a crazy-quilting project leaves you uncertain about where, or how, to begin, look no further! These crazy-pieced charmers are like no other crazy quilting you've encountered! We've given you templates for each section of the ornament, as well as placement indications for each fabric piece. With the easy, step-by-step instructions, you'll be ready to get started right away. Choose brights or pastels and get set for crazy-quilting fun!

Note: For these projects, a general materials list and instructions have been given. Specific materials and instructions for each project have been listed separately.

General materials:
¼ yd. lightweight interfacing (makes six ornaments)
Embroidery floss **or** size 5 pearl cotton to match fabrics
Thread to match fabrics
Polyester filling
Freezer paper
Hand-sewing needle
Straight pins
Scissors
Iron
Sewing machine

General instructions:
1. Cut ornament shape from foundation fabric. (**Note:** A ¼" seam allowance is included in pattern.)
2. Baste shape to lightweight interfacing and trim interfacing to fit shape.
3. Cut 1½" x 4½" strips from contrasting fabrics. Apply strips to

ornaments in order indicated by numbers on pattern. Place strip right-side down atop foundation fabric, aligning edge of strip with line on pattern and placing bulk of strip toward inside of ornament. Sew using a ¼" seam allowance. Press along seam line. Pin strip flat to foundation fabric and trim away excess strip fabric from wrong side of ornament.

4. For basket appliqué, cut freezer paper to exact size of basket pattern. Iron freezer paper shiny-side down to back side of basket fabric. Cut around freezer paper, adding a ¼" seam allowance. Fold seam allowance to back side of appliqué, baste in place, and press along edge. Blind stitch basket to ornament, leaving a ¾" opening along one side. Remove basting stitches and freezer paper and sew opening closed. Press.

5. Work decorative stitching along seam lines, using size 5 pearl cotton or four strands embroidery floss in contrasting colors and referring to photos for stitch placement. Stitches used for models are: chain stitch, lazy-daisy stitch, buttonhole stitch, backstitch, cross stitch, star stitch, and French knots.

6. Work silk-ribbon embroidery using straight stitch for stems and small buds and lazy-daisy stitch for leaves and flowers.

Jewel-Tone Ornaments
Materials:
¼ yd. black cotton fabric (for foundation and backing)
1½" x 4½" fabric strips (**Note:** Cut five from red print, three from blue print, three from gold print, and four from green print.)
3" x 5" scrap brown-print fabric
2mm dark-green silk ribbon
2mm red silk ribbon

Square Ornament
1. Prepare foundation fabric referring to general instructions.
2. Sew gold strip in place at area 1. Sew blue strip in place at area 2. Sew red strips in place at areas 3 and 4. Sew green strips in place at areas 5 and 6.
3. Appliqué basket #1 to center of ornament, placing bottom of basket 1" up from bottom edge of ornament.
4. Work silk-ribbon embroidery across top of basket. Add decorative stitching.

Heart Ornament
1. Prepare foundation fabric referring to general instructions.
2. Sew red strips in place at areas 1 and 2. Sew blue strip in place at area 3. Sew green strip in place at area 4. Sew gold strip in place at area 5.
3. Work silk-ribbon embroidery on black center. Add decorative stitching.

Octagon Ornament
1. Prepare foundation fabric referring to general instructions.
2. Sew gold strip in place at area 1. Sew red strip in place at area 2. Sew blue strip in place at area 3. Sew green strip in place at area 4.
3. Appliqué basket #2 to center of ornament, placing bottom of basket 1⅜" up from bottom edge of ornament.
4. Work silk-ribbon embroidery across top of basket. Add decorative stitching.

Pastel Ornaments
Materials:
¼ yd. ivory-print cotton fabric (for foundation and backing)
1½" x 4½" fabric strips (**Note:** Cut four from pink plaid, three from blue print, four from lavender print, and four from green print.)
3" x 5" scrap light-brown fabric
4mm light-green silk ribbon
4mm pink silk ribbon

Square Ornament
1. Prepare foundation fabric referring to general instructions.
2. Sew blue strip in place at area 1. Sew pink strip in place at area 2. Sew green strips in place at areas 3 and 4. Sew lavender strips in place at areas 5 and 6.
3. Appliqué basket #1 to center of ornament, placing bottom of basket 1" up from bottom edge of ornament.
4. Work silk-ribbon embroidery across top of basket. Add decorative stitching.

Heart Ornament
1. Prepare foundation fabric referring to general instructions.
2. Sew pink strips in place at areas 1 and 2. Sew blue strip in place at area 3. Sew green strip in place at area 4. Sew lavender strip in place at area 5.
3. Work silk-ribbon embroidery on ivory-print center. Add decorative stitching.

Octagon Ornament
1. Prepare foundation fabric referring to general instructions.
2. Sew pink strip in place at area 1. Sew lavender strip in place at area 2. Sew blue strip in place at area 3. Sew green strip in place at area 4.
3. Appliqué basket #2 to center of ornament, placing bottom of basket 1⅜" up from bottom edge of ornament.
4. Work silk-ribbon embroidery across top of basket. Add decorative stitching.

Finishing:
Turn to page **131** for "Basic Ornament-Finishing Instructions."

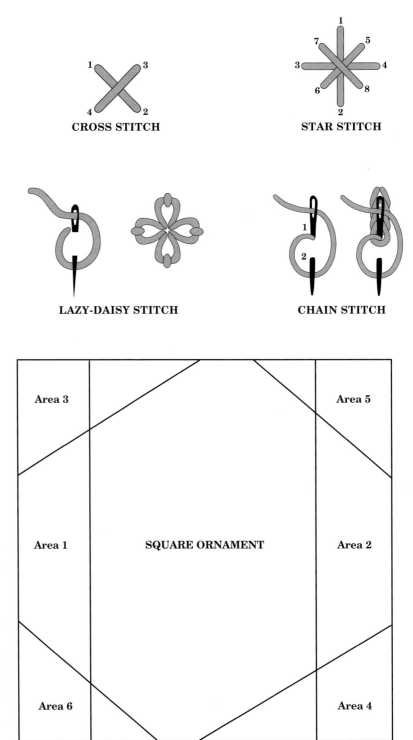

CROSS STITCH

STAR STITCH

LAZY-DAISY STITCH

CHAIN STITCH

SQUARE ORNAMENT

Area 3
Area 5
Area 1
Area 2
Area 6
Area 4

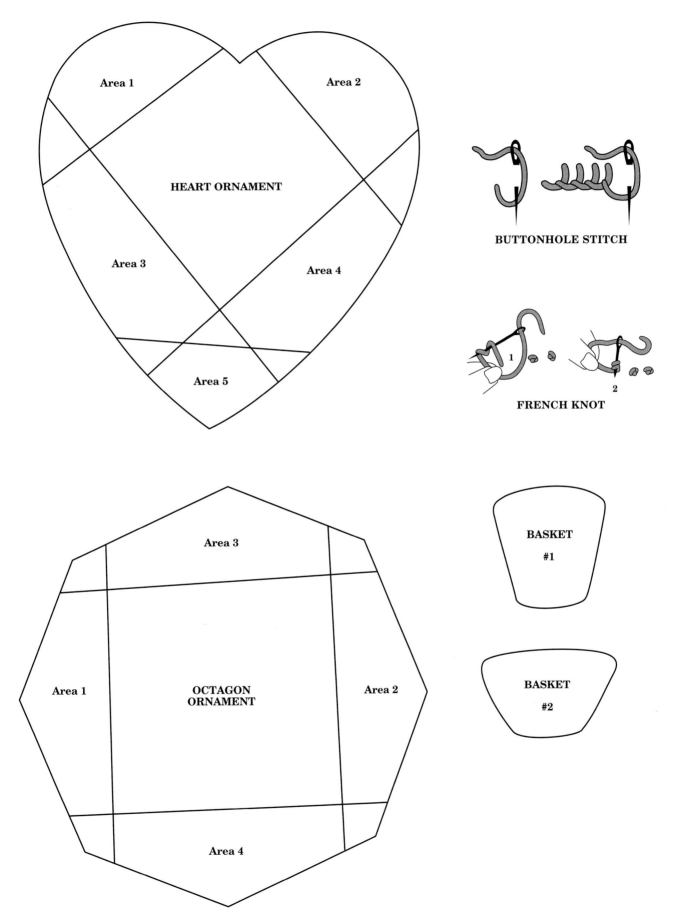

HEART ORNAMENT

Area 1

Area 2

Area 3

Area 4

Area 5

BUTTONHOLE STITCH

FRENCH KNOT

OCTAGON ORNAMENT

Area 3

Area 1

Area 2

Area 4

BASKET #1

BASKET #2

Silk-Ribbon
Ball Ornaments

Silk-ribbon embroidery, one of the most-popular needlecrafts around, was used to create this sextet of gorgeous ornaments. Splendid for display across a mantel, or on a Christmas tree that is decorated to boast Victorian flair, these pieces will make wonderful additions to your holiday decorating. Finish them with ivory lace trim and ribbons, and be prepared for compliments.

YLI Silk Ribbon

☐ 3	white	(7mm)
☐ 13	yellow	(2mm)
☐ 32	green, med.	(4mm)
▨ 33	green, dk.	(4mm)
☐ 68	pink	(2mm)
■ 70	fuchsia	(2mm)
▨ 101	lavender	(7mm)
▨ 128	mauve	(7mm)

DMC	Color
white	white
676	old gold, lt.
563	jade, lt.

Mill Hill Petite Glass Beads

40123	cream
42011	Victorian gold

Fabric: Burgundy and teal taffeta fabric. (Cut fabric 14" x 11".)

ORNAMENT DIAGRAM

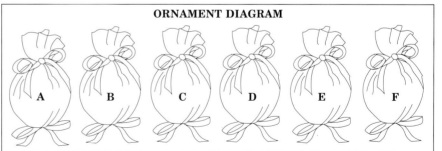

A   B   C   D   E   F

Note: Use of an embroidery hoop is recommended for these projects.

Stem stitch—Work vines using two strands DMC 563. Work stems using one strand DMC 563.

◖ **Japanese ribbon stitch**

✪ **French knot using ribbon**

○ **Glass bead**

Feather stitch—Work using one strand 563. Attach gold bead at ends.

Pistil stitch—Work using one strand 676. Attach gold bead at ends.

Straight-Stitch rose

Side ribbon-stitch rose

Plume stitch with French knot

Lazy-daisy stitch with fly stitch

Lazy-daisy stitch with French knot in center

Bow—Couch as indicated on pattern.

Finishing instructions:
Materials:
One 3" STYROFOAM brand plastic foam ball (for **each** ornament)
11" length ¾"-wide ivory lace trim (for **each** ornament)
30" length ¼"-wide ivory satin ribbon (for **each** ornament)
Thread to match fabric and trim
Hand-sewing needle
Scissors
Sewing machine (optional)

1. Complete stitching following instructions given.
2. Trim fabric from bottom edge of design, leaving 2½" of fabric below design.
3. Measure up 6⅝" from bottom edge of fabric, and trim.
4. Trim width of fabric to 11", centering design.
5. Turn bottom edge of fabric under 1", and sew a gathering stitch ¼" from edge.
6. Place lace at top edge of fabric, overlapping ¼", and zigzag lace to fabric.
7. Pull up gathering thread at bottom of fabric, and place fabric around Styrofoam® ball. Gather bottom tightly to cover ball, and knot thread to secure.
8. Place fabric around ball, and hand sew seam in back, folding edge of overlapping fabric under for a neat finish.
9. At top of ball, gather fabric tightly with 12" length of ribbon, tying a knot in ribbon to secure, and tying remaining length of ribbon in a bow.
10. Tie a bow in 10" length of ribbon, and tack bow at bottom of ball.
11. Fold 8" length of ribbon in half to form loop, knotting ribbon ends together to secure. Tack loop to back side of ornament, attaching to gathering ribbon at top of ornament.

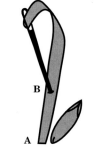

JAPANESE RIBBON STITCH

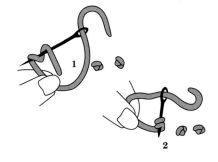

FRENCH KNOT

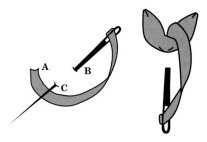

FLY STITCH

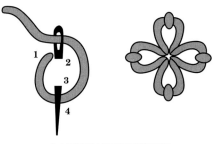

LAZY-DAISY STITCH

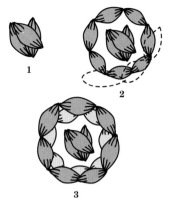

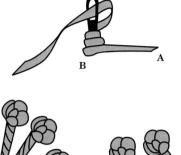

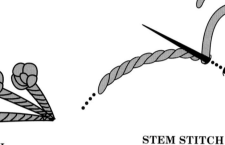

STRAIGHT-STITCH ROSE

Start in the center with a straight stitch angled to the right. Overlay second straight stitch to cover top of first stitch. Cover base of second stitch with third straight stitch, angling this stitch to the left. Circle center piece with seven straight stitches. Circle around in a second row, overlapping previous row and overlapping joining points of first row with the longer straight stitch of the second row.

PISTIL STITCH

Bring needle up at A and form a French knot at the end of a short length of ribbon or thread. Take needle down at B (the length away from A of the thread plus French knot), and pull firmly into place.

STEM STITCH

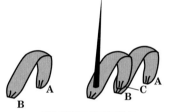

PLUME STITCH

Bring needle up at A and go down ⅛" away at B, keeping ribbon flat at all times. Make a loop. Hold loop in place with thumb and bring needle up at C, piercing fabric and ribbon. Form another loop. Continue down until plume is finished.

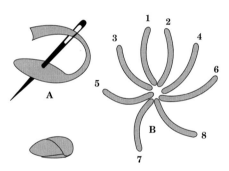

SIDE-RIBBON-STITCH ROSE

Work petals in a loose side ribbon stitch. See Illustration A. Place petals according to numbers, taking needle down at each number. See Illustration B.

FEATHER STITCH

TOP

ORNAMENT A

TOP

ORNAMENT B

TOP

ORNAMENT C

96

TOP

ORNAMENT D

TOP

ORNAMENT E

TOP

ORNAMENT F

97

Quilters' Delights

We've combined traditional quilting patterns with a variety of color schemes to create these quilted charmers. The Traditional Nine-Patch Ornaments *feature the ever-popular Spool, Windmill, and Shoo Fly designs, and the* Gold-Accented Ornaments *are embellished with bugle beads. Make these tiny, quilted treasures and rest assured they will delight the quilting enthusiasts who visit in your home this holiday season.*

Traditional Nine-Patch Ornaments

Note: For these projects, a general materials list has been given. Specific materials for each project have been listed separately.

General materials:
Muslin (**Note:** A 4" square is required for **each** ornament.)
Lightweight quilt batting
7" length matching embroidery floss **or** narrow ribbon for **each** ornament (for hanger)
Thread to match fabrics
Hand-sewing needle
Measuring tape
Pencil
Scissors
Iron

Finished size: 3" square

Shoo Fly
Four 1½" squares green-print fabric
Two 1⅞" squares green-print fabric, cut in half diagonally to make four triangles
One 1½" square red-print fabric
Two 1⅞" squares red-and-white print fabric, cut in half diagonally to make four triangles
Complementary fabric (for backing)

Spool
Two 1½" squares blue-and-white print fabric
Two 1⅞" squares blue-and-white print fabric, cut in half diagonally to make four triangles
One 1½" square blue-print fabric

Two 1½" squares mustard-print fabric
Two 1⅞" squares mustard-print fabric, cut in half diagonally to make four triangles
Complementary fabric (for backing)

Windmill
Four 1⅞" squares blue-print fabric, cut in half diagonally to make eight triangles
One 1½" square mustard-print fabric
Two 1⅞" squares red-print fabric, cut in half diagonally to make four triangles
Two 1⅞" squares green-print fabric, cut in half diagonally to make four triangles
Complementary fabric (for backing)

1. Piece ornament front, referring to diagrams for assembly and using a ¼" seam allowance.
2. Cut squares of muslin and batting slightly larger than pieced front.
3. Place pieced front atop muslin and batting. Hand or machine quilt around design as desired.
4. Trim away excess muslin and batting.
5. Place quilted ornament face-down atop larger piece of backing fabric, and sew around perimeter, using a ¼" seam allowance and leaving an opening for turning.
6. Trim away excess backing fabric. Turn piece to right side, press along edges, and whipstitch opening closed.
7. Tack 7"-length looped embroidery floss or narrow ribbon at top center of ornament to form hanger.

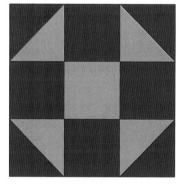

SHOO FLY

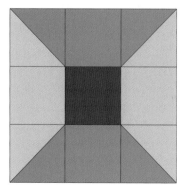

SPOOL

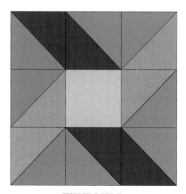

WINDMILL

Gold-Accented Ornaments

Note: For these projects, a general materials list has been given. Specific materials for each project have been listed separately.

General materials:
Muslin (**Note:** A 4" square is required for **each** ornament.)
Lightweight quilt batting
11 small gold bugle beads
21" gold braid, cut into 7" lengths (for hangers)
Thread to match fabrics
Hand-sewing needle
Measuring tape
Pencil
Scissors
Iron

Finished size: 3" square

Nine-Patch Star
Four 1½" squares solid-pink fabric
Two 1⅞" squares solid-pink fabric, cut in half diagonally to make four triangles
One 1½" square pink-and-burgundy metallic-print fabric
Two 1⅞" squares pink-and-burgundy metallic-print fabric, cut in half diagonally to make four triangles
Complementary fabric (for backing)

Maple Leaf
Two 1½" squares solid-blue fabric
Two 1⅞" squares solid-blue fabric, cut in half diagonally to make four triangles
Three 1½" squares brown-and-blue metallic-print fabric
Two 1⅞" squares brown-and-blue metallic-print fabric, cut in half diagonally to make four triangles
One 1¾" x ¾" bias strip brown-and-blue metallic-print fabric
Complementary fabric (for backing)

Pinwheel
Two 2⅜" squares solid-green fabric, cut in half diagonally to make four triangles
Two 2⅜" squares green-and-pink metallic-print fabric, cut in half diagonally to make four triangles
Complementary fabric (for backing)

1. Piece ornament front referring to diagrams for assembly and using a ¼" seam allowance.
2. Cut squares of muslin and batting slightly larger than pieced front.
3. Place pieced front atop muslin and batting. Hand or machine quilt around design as desired.
4. Trim away excess muslin and batting.
5. Add small, gold bugle beads where indicated on diagram.
6. Place quilted ornament face-down atop larger piece of backing fabric, and sew around perimeter, using a ¼" seam allowance and leaving an opening for turning.
7. Trim away excess backing fabric. Turn piece to right side, press along edges, and whipstitch opening closed.
8. Tack 7"-length looped gold braid at top corner of ornament to form hanger.

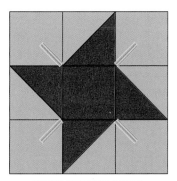

NINE-PATCH STAR

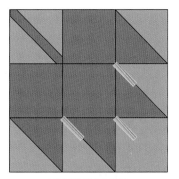

MAPLE LEAF

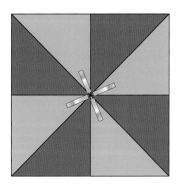

PINWHEEL

Tassel Treasures

Sometimes the smallest touches can help transform a house into a well-decorated home. In this busiest of seasons, set aside a little time for making these attractive tassels; then use them as drapery tiebacks, hang them from drawer pulls or doorknobs, or suspend them from the branches of your Christmas tree. They can even be used as package trimming that becomes part of the gift!

*From Left—*Violet Tassel *and* Blue Tassel

Note: For these projects, a general materials list and instructions have been given. Specific materials and instructions for each project have been listed separately.

Basic Tassels

General materials:
5½"-long piece sturdy cardboard
4"-long piece sturdy cardboard
Hand-sewing needle
Tapestry needle
Scissors

General instructions:
Note: Illustrations are on page **103.** Wrap fibers around 5½"-long piece of sturdy cardboard to desired thickness, referring to Illustration 1. Slip tie under cardboard at top of tassel; tie tightly. See Illustration 2. Remove from cardboard. Wrap second thread around neck of tassel. See Illustration 3. Wrap thread tails around tie, referring to Illustration 4, and bury end in tassel. Cut along bottom of tassel through all fibers. If desired, insert bead into head of tassel to add fullness.

White Button Tassels *and* **Royal-Blue Button Tassels**

From Left—Harlequin Tassel *and* Golden-Crown Tassel

From Left—Mini-Crown Tassel, Wildflower Tassel, *and* Beaded Top-Knot Tassel

Blue Tassel
Materials:
One 75-yd. mini-skein 100% linen yarn from Euroflax, Inc., 034 royal blue
One 8-yd. card Rhapsody 100% nylon tubular ribbon, R17 fandango

1. Wrap royal-blue linen yarn to 75% of desired fullness.
2. Wrap 7 yds. Rhapsody and linen yarn together for remaining fullness.
3. Wrap neck to secure, using double length linen yarn. Run linen yarn through remaining Rhapsody; gather and wrap neck twice.

Violet Tassel
Materials:
One 25-m. skein **each,** size 5 DMC pearl cotton, colors: 311 navy, med.; 319 pistachio, vy. dk.; 327 violet, dk.
One 10-yd. skein Watercolours® from The Caron Collection, 006 amethyst

1. Wrap all colors at once.
2. Wrap neck to secure, using amethyst Watercolours®.
3. Work cloud filling stitch on tassel head, using amethyst Watercolours®.

Button Tassels

White Button Tassel
Materials:
anny blatt Victoria ribbon yarn, 060 blanc
1⅛"-diameter button (**Note:** Designer used JHB Bicyclist button #95080.)

1. Cut 16" length of yarn. Fold in half; tie knot 2" from fold. Thread one tail through shank on button back. Make second knot around shank. Leave ends loose to secure tassel.
2. Wrap remaining yarn around 4" piece of cardboard. Cut at one end, and tie top of tassel, with ends attached to button.
3. Knot yarn as desired for added dimension. Trim ends even.

Royal-Blue Button Tassel
Materials:
One 5-yd. reel YLI silk ribbon, 99 royal blue
¾"-diameter button (**Note:** Designer used JHB Tuileries button #90735.)

1. Cut 8" length of ribbon. Wrap remaining ribbon around 4" piece of

cardboard. Cut at one end, and tie 8" length of ribbon around neck of tassel.
2. Thread tie through shank on button; knot. Trim ends even.

Crown-Knot Tassels

General instructions:
Separate threads into two groups of equal size. Weave groups of threads as shown in Illustration 1. Pull threads evenly to center the knot. Weave threads to form second knot, as shown in Illustration 2. Pull downward on all threads to form tassel head. This creates the crown knot. Loosen knot slightly on head of tassel, and insert hanger. Secure hanger in knot. Smooth tassel skirt; tie neck with desired fiber. Trim tassel if desired.

Beaded Top-Knot Tassel
Materials:
One 10-yd. skein Watercolours® from The Caron Collection, 091 blue spruce
One 10-m. reel Kreinik medium (#16) braid, 1223 passion plum
One pkg. Mill Hill Pebble Beads, 05145 pale pink

102

1. Cut skein into twenty 18" lengths; separate plies.

2. Separate into two groups and tie crown knot as indicated in general instructions.

3. Make hanging cord with Kreinik braid.

4. Wrap neck of tassel directly below knot and again ½" below first wrapped neck.

5. Thread beads on outer threads of tassel; knot thread below beads, varying heights. Trim just below bead knots.

Mini-Crown Tassel
Materials:

One 8-m. skein **each** DMC embroidery floss, colors: 991 aqua, dk.; 992 aqua

One 10-m. reel Kreinik medium (#16) braid, 221 antique gold

1. Cut floss into 12" lengths.

2. Separate into two groups by color and tie crown knot as indicated in general instructions.

3. Make twisted-cord hanger in color desired, referring to "How-tos for Making Twisted Cording" on page **141.**

4. Wrap neck with gold braid.

Harlequin Tassel
Materials:

Two 5-m. mini-skeins **each** Kreinik Soie d'Alger, colors: noir (black), blanc (white)

One 3-m. skein black Kreinik Facets™

1. Open skeins and cut through knotted end of loop. Set aside one length black for twisted-cord hanger.

2. Separate into two groups by color and tie crown knot as indicated in general instructions.

3. Make twisted-cord hanger in black, referring to "How-tos for Making Twisted Cording" on page **141.** Insert into tassel.

4. Wrap neck with Facets™.

Wildflower Tassel
Materials:

Two 5-m. mini-skeins Kreinik Soie d'Alger, 135 aqua, dk.

One 10-m. reel Kreinik medium (#16) braid, 202HL Aztec gold

One 36-yd. skein Wildflowers® from The Caron Collection, 089 Caribbean

1. Open skeins of Soie d'Alger and cut through knotted end of loop. Combine skeins into one group.

2. Cut Wildflowers® into 18" lengths.

3. Tie crown knot as indicated in general instructions.

4. Make twisted-cord hanger from braid, referring to "How-tos for Making Twisted Cording" on page **141.**

5. Wrap neck with braid.

Golden-Crown Tassel
Materials:

One 43-yd. skein Kreinik Soie d'Alger, noir (black)

⅔ yd. #50 gold Kreinik Torsade

One pkg. AK Designs beads, 809 gold

1. Open skein of Soie d'Alger and cut through knotted end of loop. Separate out four, 8-thread bundles and cut into 13" lengths.

2. Fold bundles in half and tie top.

3. Cut Torsade into 12" lengths, taping ends before cutting. Make crown knot as indicated in general instructions.

4. Make twisted cord using one cut length of silk thread, referring to "How-tos for Making Twisted Cording" on page **141.**

5. Bind cut ends of Torsade with silk thread and sew together to secure.

6. Sew silk tassels to bottom of knot, hiding bound edges of knot and tassel stitches.

7. Wrap neck of tassel with silk thread, wrapping 1" from knot.

8. Sew beads around wrapped neck, using one strand silk thread.

CROWN–KNOT TASSELS

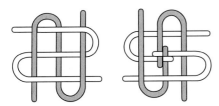

ILLUSTRATION 1   ILLUSTRATION 2

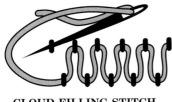

CLOUD FILLING STITCH

BASIC TASSELS

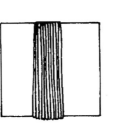

ILLUSTRATION 1   ILLUSTRATION 2   ILLUSTRATION 3

ILLUSTRATION 4

COMPLETED TASSEL

Counterchange Smocked Ornaments

Most of us envision embellishments on children's clothing when we think of smocking. But these Counterchange Smocked Ornaments *offer a wonderful way to use this age-old needleart in an unexpected manner! Make this trio in the pastel shades shown or, if you prefer, craft them using traditional holiday colors.*

Materials:

2½" STYROFOAM brand plastic foam ball (for **each** small ornament)

3" STYROFOAM brand plastic foam ball (for large ornament)

One 19" x 4" piece striped fabric (for **each** small ornament)

One 25" x 4⅞" piece striped fabric (for large ornament) (**Note:** Stripes are ¼" wide.)

Silk ribbon in assorted colors of your choice

¼"-wide satin ribbon in assorted colors of your choice

Embroidery floss to match fabrics

Thread to match fabrics

Water-soluble marker or quilter's pencil

Tacky glue

Silk flowers

Small pieces fine wire

#7 darning needle (for smocking)

Hand-sewing needle

Straight pins

Scissors

Iron

Ironing board

Note: Counterchange smocking does not require pre-pleating. Each square on chart represents one, ¼"-square area. Fabric stripes are indicated by stripes on chart. Design has an eight-stripe repeat.

1. Draw lines perpendicular to the stripes on the fabric, using marker or quilter's pencil.

2. Centering design on fabric, work design in half- and full-cable stitches, using three strands coordinating floss and working from left to right. **Note:** Work Rows 2 and 3 **only** for small ornaments and all four rows for large ornament.

3. Wash away markings. Block smocked piece by pinning piece to ironing board and pulling fabric vertically to close pleats. Press gently with iron, using steam.

4. If desired, work floral design centered in large, diamond-shaped areas. Work a cluster of twelve various-colored French knots, using silk ribbon. Work three lazy-daisy stitches for leaves.

5. Turn under ⅛" on one short edge of panel; baste. Pin panel to Styrofoam® ball at opposite short edge. Pin along top edge, turning under as you go. Repeat along bottom edge. Overlap short edges, placing turned-under edge on top. Hand sew pleats together at top and bottom, overlapping pleats like a fan. Hand sew back seam together.

6. Make hanging loop from silk ribbon. Dip point of pin in tacky glue, and pin loop to top of ornament. Glue embellishments to top and bottom of ornament as desired, using satin-ribbon flowers, silk-ribbon leaves, silk ribbon, and silk flowers.

To make satin-ribbon flowers:
Cut a 2" length of ¼"-wide ribbon. Sew cut edges together, using a ⅛" seam allowance. Sew running stitch along one edge of loop; pull to gather. Sew gathers in place to secure.

To make satin-ribbon leaves:
Make a loop of ribbon and sew or glue cut ends together.

To make silk-ribbon ferns:
Wrap lengths of ribbon around small pieces of wire, gluing in place and layering as desired.

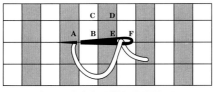

CABLE STITCH (STEP 1)

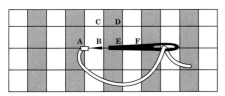

CABLE STITCH (STEP 2)

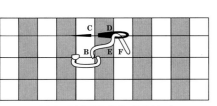

CABLE STITCH (STEP 3)

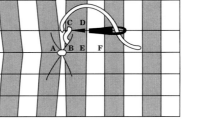

CABLE STITCH (STEP 4)

CABLE STITCH (STEP 5)

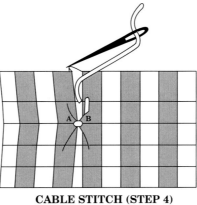

CABLE STITCH (STEP 6)

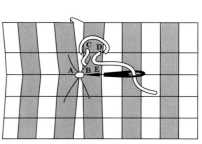

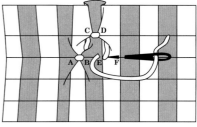

CABLE STITCH (STEP 6)

CABLE STITCH (STEP 7)

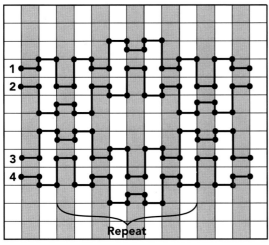

SMOCKING CHART

FRENCH KNOT

LAZY-DAISY STITCH

Five Golden Rings

Season's Craftings

We know that there are many handicrafters out there who take a special liking to projects with a "crafty" flair. With that in mind, we have gathered an assortment of design ideas that requires a variety of techniques and handiworking skills. Whether your favorites include heartwarming appliqué with traditional holiday motifs and colors, unique creations made from attic treasures and sewing-basket scraps, or the irresistible Twelve Days of Christmas ornaments, you're certain to find just the right ideas to make this year's decorating and gift planning as much fun as the Christmas season itself!

Twelve Days of Christmas

Who could forget that favorite carol, "The Twelve Days of Christmas"? This set of ornaments brings this yuletide classic to life in an unforgettable way. The mantel provides a wonderful place to display this eye-catching dozen, which combines crafting techniques with hand sewing and beading. From twelve drummers drumming to a partridge in a pear tree, these pieces are certain to delight you and yours this holiday season!

Note: For these projects, a general materials list and instructions have been given. Specific materials and instructions for each project have been listed separately.

General materials:
Felt, colors: light gold, dark gold, olive green, bright green, rust, tan, pink, light turquoise, turquoise, light blue, medium blue, dark blue, navy, pale yellow, bright yellow, black, red, maroon, white, orange, rose, gray, light purple, dark purple, peach flesh, dark brown
Seed beads: one package assorted colors, one package crystal

3 x 6mm pearl beads
5mm sequins, colors: red, gold, white, rose, blue, green, turquoise, bronze, black
1/16"-thick basswood (cut twelve 1¼" x 4" pieces for bases)
Metallic-gold acrylic paint
Gold glitter
Thick tacky glue
Thread to match felt
7" length metallic-gold thread (for **each** ornament)
Hand-sewing needle
Black permanent-ink pen
Tracing paper
Pencil
Straight pins
Small sharp scissors

1. Paint basswood bases with metallic-gold acrylic paint. Let dry.
2. Assemble all figures completely before attaching to base.
Note: When directions state "Cut two bodies," cut entire figure. Smaller pieces are then cut and glued in place.
3. To attach sequins, bring needle up through back of felt, pick up sequin and a crystal bead, and sew back through sequin hole and felt.
Note: When a project calls for beads other than crystal, the colors and/or types needed have been included in the instructions for that project.
4. After figure has been glued to base, sequins may be glued to base, if desired.

5. Print titles across bases ¼" from bottom, using black, permanent-ink pen.

6. Thread needle with a 7" length of metallic-gold thread. Draw through top center of figure and tie a knot in thread ends to form hanger.

Partridge in a Pear Tree
Materials:
One 1½" x 2½" piece gold felt
One 1½" x 2½" piece olive-green felt
Two 4½" x 5" pieces rust felt
One 1¾" x 2¾" piece tan felt

1. Cut four olive-green leaves, two gold pears, one gold beak, one tan wing, and two rust bodies.
2. Place the two body pieces together and whipstitch around edges. Repeat for leaves and pear.
3. Glue wing and beak to body, as indicated on pattern.
4. Sew gold sequins where *X* appears on pattern. Sew bronze sequins where *O* appears on pattern.
5. Glue pear and bird to base. Print title.
6. Attach hanger.

Two Turtle Doves
Materials:
Two 3½" x 4" pieces red felt
Four 2½" x 3" pieces medium-blue felt
Two 1½" x 1¾" pieces dark-blue felt
Scrap of pale-yellow felt

1. Cut two red hearts, four medium-blue bodies, two dark-blue wings, and two pale-yellow beaks.
2. Whipstitch edges of hearts together and attach red sequins where *X* appears on pattern.
3. Whipstitch bodies together. Glue on wings and beaks as indicated on pattern.
4. Sew pearl beads at top of each head.
5. Sew blue sequins where *O* appears on pattern.
6. Glue birds to heart, facing each other.
7. Glue heart to base. Print title.
8. Attach hanger.

Three French Hens
Materials:
Three 1" x 1½" pieces pink felt
Six 2½" squares dark-blue felt

Scrap of red felt
Scrap of gold felt

1. Cut three pink wings, six dark-blue bodies, three gold beaks, three red combs, and three red wattles.
2. Whipstitch edges of bodies together to make three hens. Glue a wing, a comb, a wattle, and a beak to each hen, as indicated on pattern.
3. Sew red sequins where + appears on pattern. Sew gold sequin where *O* appears on pattern. Sew rose sequins on two hens where *X* appears on pattern. On third hen, sew rose sequins all the way around the wing, and add a second row of sequins along bottom of wing.
4. Glue three hens together; then glue to base. Print title.
5. Attach hanger.

Four Calling Birds
Materials:
Eight 2" x 4" pieces maroon felt
Four 1½" x 1¾" pieces white felt
Scrap of gold felt

1. Cut four white wings, four gold beaks, and eight maroon bodies.
2. Whipstitch bodies together to make four birds. Glue beaks and wings to each bird, as indicated on pattern.
3. Sew four gold beads along beak. Sew a white sequin on each bird for eye, using a gold bead. Outline each wing with white sequins, using red beads.
4. Glue four birds together; then glue to base. Print title.
5. Attach hanger.

Five Golden Rings
Materials:
Five 1" plastic rings
Gold glitter
Paper plate
Plastic wrap

1. Working over a paper plate, coat one side and edges of rings with glue. Sprinkle with glitter. Place on plastic wrap to dry.
2. Glue three rings along top of base. Glue remaining two rings pyramid style on top of first three rings.
3. Print title.
4. Attach hanger.

Six Geese A-Laying
Materials:
Two 3½" x 4¼" pieces pale-yellow felt
One 1½" x 2½" piece light-turquoise felt
Scrap of orange felt
Scrap of white felt

1. Cut two yellow bodies, one turquoise wing, one orange beak, and three white eggs.
2. Whipstitch body together. Glue on beak and wing, as indicated on pattern.
3. Sew five crystal beads along top of beak. Sew gold sequins where *O* appears on pattern. Sew turquoise sequins where *X* appears on pattern. Sew three pearl beads to each egg.
4. Glue goose and eggs to base. Print title.
5. Attach hanger.

Seven Swans A-Swimming
Materials:
Two 4¼" x 5" pieces white felt
One 2" x 3½" piece white felt
Scrap of black felt

1. Cut two white bodies, one white wing, and one black beak.
2. Whipstitch body pieces together. Glue wing and beak to body, as indicated on pattern.
3. Sew gold sequins where *X* appears on pattern. Sew five gold beads on beak, as indicated on pattern. Sew two pearl beads along top of beak. Sew black sequin for eye.
4. Glue swan to base. Print title.
5. Attach hanger.

Eight Maids A-Milking
Materials:
Two 3" x 5" pieces rose felt
Two 2½" x 3¼" pieces dark-blue felt
One 1¼" square peach flesh felt
One 1" x 1¼" piece light-gold felt
One 1" square gray felt
Scrap of rust felt
Scrap of white felt
Gray embroidery floss

1. Cut two bodies from rose felt. Whipstitch edges together. Set aside.
2. Cut one bonnet, one bow, and one dress border from dark-blue felt. Cut two sleeves from rose felt; two hands and one face from peach-flesh

felt; hair from light-gold felt; two shoes from rust felt; one pail from gray felt; and one inside area of pail from white felt.

Note: Cut pieces slightly larger than pattern.

3. Place pieces atop stitched body to check for fit. Trim if necessary.

4. Glue pieces to body in following order: shoes, dress border, hands, sleeves, face, hair, bonnet, bow, pail, and inside area of pail.

5. To make pail handle, bring needle threaded with six strands of gray floss up through one side of pail, under hand, and down through opposite side of pail.

6. Sew blue sequins along top of dress border and at bottom of each sleeve. Sew crystal beads along top of pail, below white felt. Sew gold beads along hairline. Sew blue and green beads along inside edge of bonnet.

7. Make eyes with ink pen.

8. Glue maid to base. Print title.

9. Attach hanger.

Nine Ladies Dancing
Materials:
Two 3½" x 5½" pieces peach-flesh felt
One 2" square dark-purple felt
One 1¾" x 2¼" piece dark-purple felt
One 2½" x 3½" piece light-purple felt
One 1½" square light-gold felt
Scrap of dark-gold felt
2½" length ⅛"-wide rose satin ribbon

1. Cut two bodies from peach-flesh felt. Whipstitch edges together. Set aside.

2. Cut two shoes from dark-gold felt; one underskirt, one bow, and one blouse from dark-purple felt; one overskirt from light-purple felt, and hair from light-gold felt.

Note: Cut pieces slightly larger than pattern.

3. Place pieces atop stitched body to check for fit. Trim if necessary.

4. Glue pieces to body in following order: shoes, underskirt, blouse, overskirt, hair, and bow. Glue ribbon around waistline.

5. Sew rose sequins along edge of overskirt and on bow. Sew rose beads along bottom of underskirt, bottom of sleeves, and neckline. Sew gold beads along hairline, and in three rows, on hair, below bow, for curls.

6. Make eyes with ink pen.

7. Glue lady to base. Print title.

8. Attach hanger.

Ten Lords A-Leaping
Materials:
Two 4½" x 6" pieces bright-green felt
One 3" x 4" piece bright-yellow felt
One 1" x 1½" piece rust felt
One 1½" square peach-flesh felt
Scrap of black felt

1. Cut two bodies from bright-green felt. Whipstitch edges together. Set aside.

2. Cut two shoes from black felt; one shirt and one cap from bright-yellow felt; two hands and one face from peach-flesh felt; and hair from rust felt.

Note: Cut pieces slightly larger than pattern.

3. Place pieces atop stitched body to check for fit. Trim if necessary.

4. Glue pieces to body in following order: hands, face, hair, cap, shirt, and shoes.

5. Sew green sequins where *X* appears on pattern. Sew gold beads where *O* appears on pattern. Sew green beads along bottom edge of cap and at waistline.

6. Make eyes with ink pen.

7. Glue lord to base. Print title.

8. Attach hanger.

Eleven Pipers Piping
Materials:
Two 3" x 5½" pieces light-blue felt
One 2" x 2½" piece turquoise felt
Two 1" x 2" pieces gold felt
Scrap of rust felt
Scrap of peach-flesh felt
Scrap of black felt

1. Cut two bodies from light-blue felt. Whipstitch edges together. Set aside.

2. Cut two horns from gold felt. Glue together. Set aside.

3. Cut two shoes from rust felt; one cap and one tunic from turquoise felt; hair from black felt; one sleeve from light-blue felt; and one hand and one face from peach-flesh felt.

Note: Cut pieces slightly larger than pattern.

4. Place pieces atop stitched body to check for fit. Trim if necessary.

5. Glue pieces to body in following order: face, hands, hair, cap, tunic, sleeve, and shoes. Glue horn to back of hand.

6. Sew turquoise sequins where *X* appears on pattern. Sew gold beads where *O* appears on pattern. Sew blue beads where + appears on pattern.

7. Make eye with ink pen.

8. Glue piper to base. Print title.

9. Attach hanger.

Twelve Drummers Drumming
Materials:
Two 3½" x 6" pieces dark-blue felt
One 2½" x 3" piece red felt
One 1½" x 2" piece navy felt
Scrap of black felt
Scrap of peach-flesh felt
Scrap of gold felt
Scrap of dark-brown felt
Scrap of white felt
Toothpick   Metallic-gold thread

1. Cut two bodies from dark-blue felt. Whipstitch edges together. Set aside.

2. Cut one drum from navy felt; one center top of drum from white felt; and bands on each end of drum from gold felt.

3. Glue white top to drum, referring to pattern for placement. Glue gold bands on either end. Straight stitch a large *W* between top and bottom of drum, using metallic-gold thread. Sew a red bead at each end of stitch. Work chain stitch across each gold band, using metallic-gold thread.

4. Cut two shoes from black felt; pants, one collar, and one hat from red felt; two hands and one face from peach-flesh felt; and hair from dark-brown felt.

Note: Cut pieces slightly larger than pattern.

5. Place pieces atop stitched body to check for fit. Trim if necessary.

6. Glue pieces to body in following order: shoes, pants, face, hair, hat, collar, drum, and hands.

7. Sew red sequins where *X* appears on pattern. Sew blue beads where *O* appears on pattern. Sew gold beads where • appears on pattern.

8. Cut toothpick 1½" long and glue blue bead on end to make drumstick. Glue to back of hand.

9. Make eye with ink pen.

10. Glue drummer to base. Print title.

11. Attach hanger.

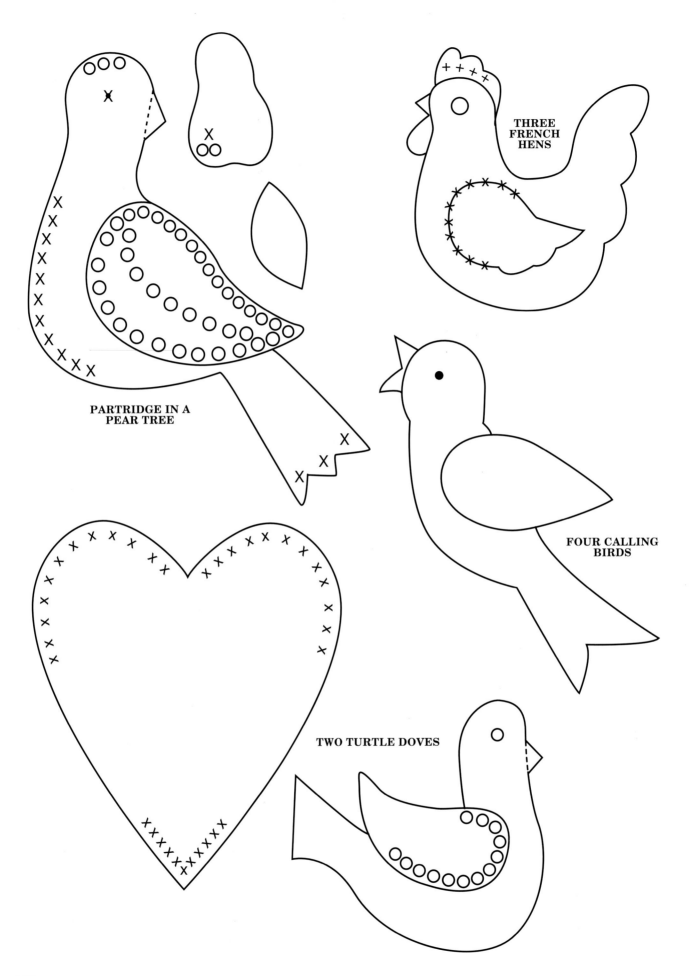

THREE
FRENCH
HENS

PARTRIDGE IN A
PEAR TREE

FOUR CALLING
BIRDS

TWO TURTLE DOVES

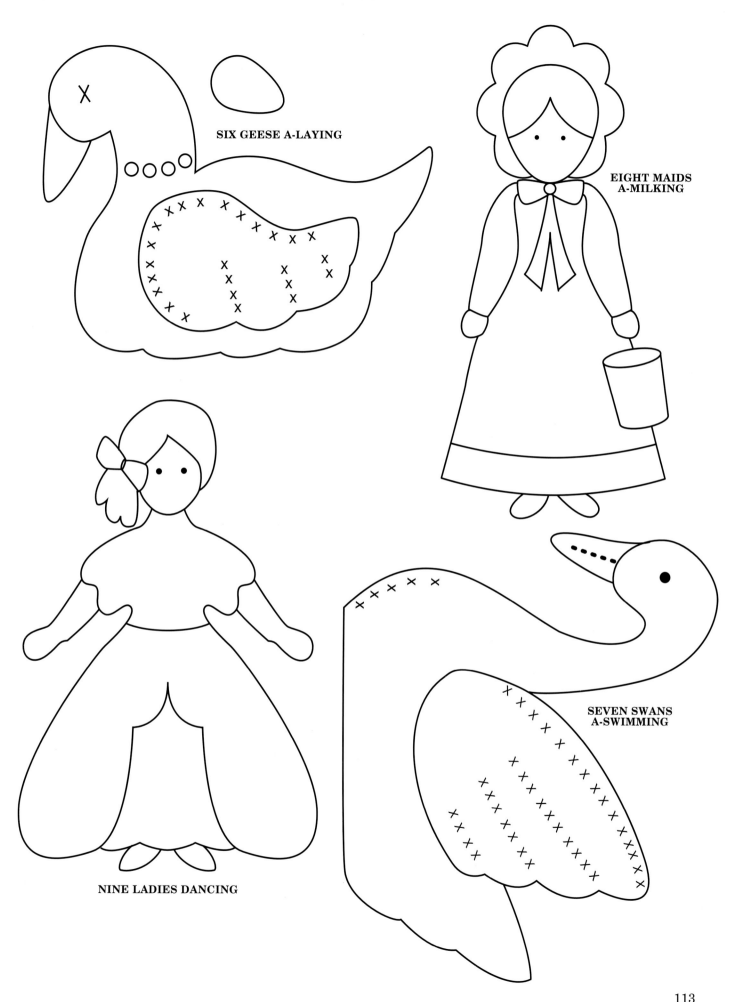

SIX GEESE A-LAYING

EIGHT MAIDS
A-MILKING

NINE LADIES DANCING

SEVEN SWANS
A-SWIMMING

113

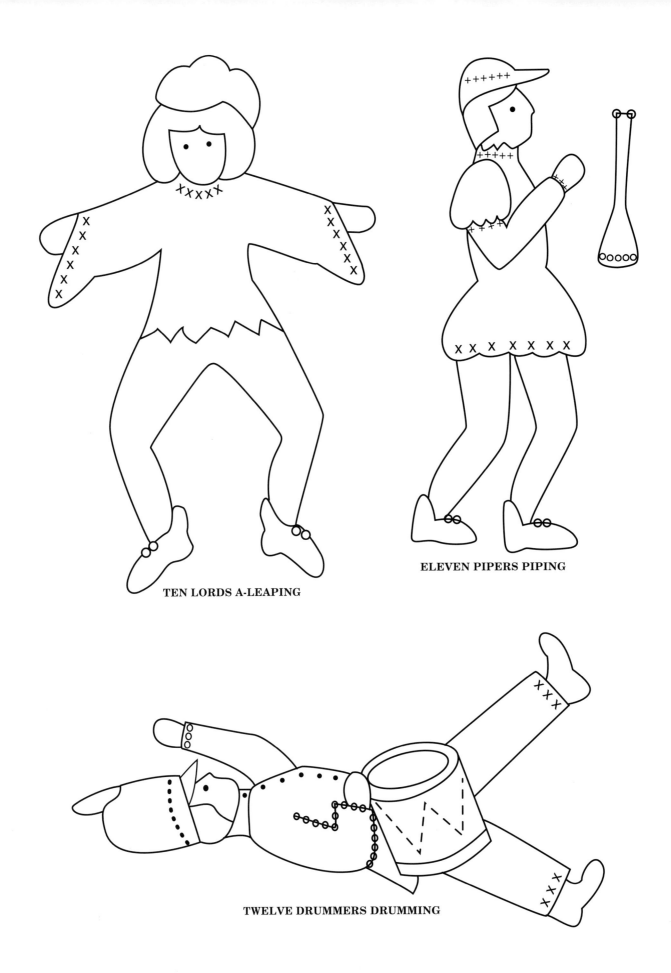

TEN LORDS A-LEAPING

ELEVEN PIPERS PIPING

TWELVE DRUMMERS DRUMMING

Quick & Easy Bazaar Ornaments

This group of designs offers a fantastic solution to the dilemma of not wanting to discard any of those leftovers in your sewing basket. Made from scraps combined with crafting items such as a glass ball ornament or a small embroidery hoop, these pieces will be ideal to sell as fund-raisers at your church bazaar or craft fair. Follow our lead, or take a look through your scrap bag and let your imagination do the rest!

Quick & Easy
Bazaar Ornaments

Note: For these projects, a general materials list has been given. Specific materials for each project have been listed separately.

General materials:
Thread to match fabrics
Hand-sewing needle
Tacky glue
Pencil
Straight pins
Scissors
Sewing machine

Yo-Yo Ornament
Materials:
3" clear glass ball
Assorted scraps of green- and red-print fabrics (**Note:** Yo-yos are made using 2½" circles of fabric.)
7" length metallic-gold thread

1. Cut fourteen green-print and fifteen red-print circles.
2. To make yo-yo, turn edge under ¼" toward wrong side of fabric, and hand-sew around perimeter. Pull thread tightly to form yo-yo, and secure thread ends. Refer to yo-yo illustrations.
3. Apply glue to back of each yo-yo and place yo-yos close together on ball, alternating colors as desired.
4. Run metallic-gold thread through ornament hanger, and tie a knot in thread ends to form hanger.

Fabric Ball
Materials:
7" square dark fabric
7" square light fabric
1 yd. ⅜"-wide red satin ribbon
7" length metallic-gold thread
Polyester filling   Tracing paper

1. Trace around pattern on fabrics, and cut two light-fabric and two dark-fabric pieces.
2. Pin one dark and one light piece with right sides of fabric together, and sew along one side, using a ¼" seam allowance. Repeat for remaining two pieces. Sew two sections together, matching seams and leaving a 1½" space for turning. Clip curves and turn right-side out.
3. Stuff firmly with polyester filling and sew opening closed.
4. Glue ribbon along seam lines. Make bow and glue to center top.
5. Thread needle with gold thread, insert through top of bow, and tie a knot in thread ends to form hanger.

Embroidery Hoop with Buttons
Materials:
4" wooden embroidery hoop
11" square muslin
15" length ¾"-wide gathered ivory eyelet trim
3 large buttons
6 small buttons
Yellow embroidery floss
7" length metallic-gold thread
Green fabric-marking pen

1. Place one 6" square of muslin atop pattern and trace lightly to mark pattern on muslin.
2. Place muslin square in hoop. Arrange buttons in flower pattern. (**Note:** Screw will be at top of ornament.) Sew in place, using yellow embroidery floss.
3. Draw stems and fill in leaves, using green pen.
4. Remove fabric from hoop. Trace outer edge of bottom hoop onto remaining piece of muslin.
5. Apply glue to outside rim of bottom hoop. Replace fabric and top hoop. Pull fabric taut. When glue has

dried, trim away excess fabric. Glue muslin to back. When glue has dried, glue eyelet trim around back edge.
6. Knot gold thread around center of screw to secure, and tie a knot in thread ends to form hanger.

Painted Doily
Materials:
Small cutwork doily
7" length metallic-gold thread
Red acrylic paint
Small paintbrush
Fabric stiffener
Plastic wrap

1. Dip doily in fabric stiffener. Straighten and lay flat atop plastic wrap to dry.
2. Using small amount of paint on brush, paint over design. Let dry. Repeat for opposite side.
3. Thread needle with gold thread, insert through top edge, and tie a knot in thread ends to form hanger.

Braided Wreath
Materials:
Three 10" squares Christmas-print fabric (**Note:** Designer used three different fabrics.)
16" length ¼"-wide red satin ribbon
1¼" yds. ¼" cording

1. Cut 1¼" x 12" bias strip from each print. Fold strip lengthwise with right sides of fabric together, and sew using a ⅛" seam allowance. Turn right-side out and insert cording.
2. Lay tubes atop work surface, baste three ends together, and braid. Tack ends together to form a ring.
3. Insert 8" length of ribbon through ring, and tie a knot in ribbon ends to form hanger. Make a bow from remaining ribbon, and glue at top of wreath.

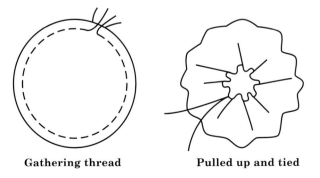

Gathering thread   Pulled up and tied

YO-YO ILLUSTRATIONS

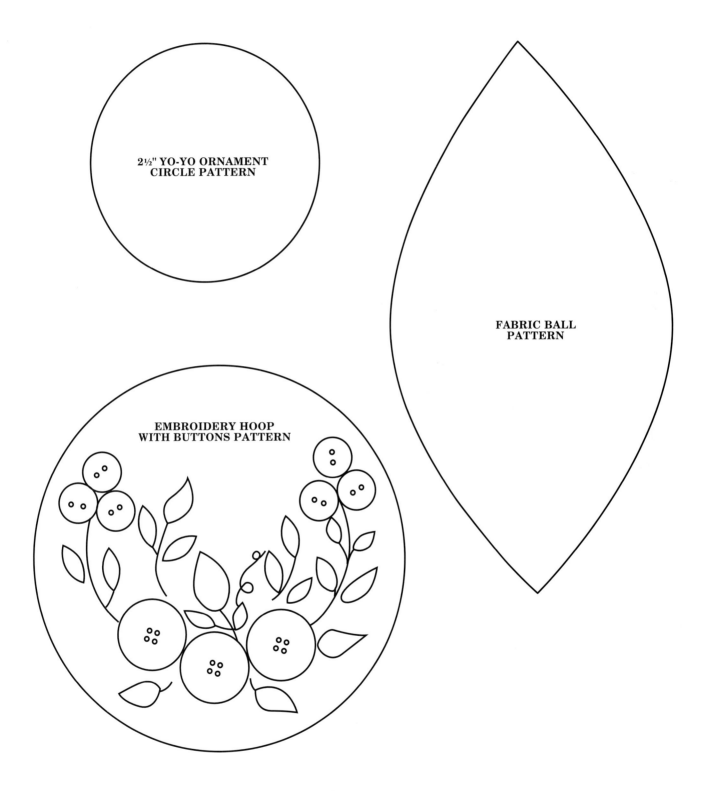

2½" YO-YO ORNAMENT
CIRCLE PATTERN

FABRIC BALL
PATTERN

EMBROIDERY HOOP
WITH BUTTONS PATTERN

Attic Crafts

Old linens and extra buttons can be given new life when you use them to create these memorable ornaments. Of course we would never suggest cutting apart heirloom linens, but tattered handkerchiefs, place mats, and other worn and torn pieces provide the perfect beginning to these projects. They also offer a fabulous way to enjoy timeless treasures for many years to come!

Note: For these projects, a general materials list has been given. Specific materials for each project have been listed separately.

General materials:
Hand-sewing needle
Scissors
Straight pins
Polyester filling
Tracing paper
Pencil

Embroidered-Handkerchief Ornament
Materials:
Handkerchief with embroidered design in each corner
3" STYROFOAM brand plastic foam ball
1 yd. ¼"-wide complementary satin ribbon
7" length metallic-gold thread
Tacky glue   Serrated knife

1. Score ball, using serrated knife and dividing ball into four sections.
2. Trace pattern onto handkerchief and cut out. Repeat three times.
3. Place one design over one fourth of ball. Push edges into ball along scored lines, using tip of knife. Repeat for remaining pieces.
4. Glue ribbon over seams. Tie a bow and glue to top of ornament.
5. Thread needle with gold thread, insert through top of bow, and tie a knot in thread ends to form hanger.

Cross-Stitched Place Mat Ornament
Materials:
Cross-stitched place mat
7" length complementary thread
Sewing machine (optional)

1. Trace pattern onto stitched area

of place mat and cut out. Repeat three times.
2. To make ball, pin two pieces of fabric with right sides together, and sew using a ¼" seam allowance. Repeat with remaining two pieces. Pin the two sections together with right sides of fabric together, matching seams, and sew, using a ¼" seam allowance and leaving a 1½" opening for turning. Clip curves and turn right-side out.
3. Stuff firmly with polyester filling and whipstitch opening closed.
4. Thread needle with thread, insert through top center of ornament, and tie a knot in thread ends to form hanger.

Lace-Covered Cone
Materials:
Two 4½" squares vintage lace
One 4½" square vintage linen
Two 4½" squares fusible web
Assorted dried **or** silk flowers
Spanish moss
7" length metallic-gold thread
Small piece STYROFOAM brand plastic foam
Hot glue gun

1. Fuse lace to either side of linen. Lightly fold two corners of square to center to form cone. Using hot glue gun, apply glue to one edge and lap other edge over glue approximately ½". Hold in place until glue sets.
2. Thread needle with gold thread, insert through back corner, and tie a knot in thread ends to form hanger.
3. Cut Styrofoam® to fit cone. Apply glue to smaller end and insert into cone. Cover with Spanish moss and glue flowers into cone.
Option: Cone can be made using vintage, linen napkin with cutwork corner.

1. Trace pattern onto napkin and cut out.
2. Fold napkin with right sides of fabric together, and sew using a ½" seam allowance. Trim seam and turn right-side out.
3. Turn top edge ½" to inside and glue. Cut designed corner of napkin into triangle, and place raw edge inside cone, adjusting to achieve desired effect. Glue raw edge in place.
4. Finish cone as for *Lace-Covered Cone,* using fruits or flowers as desired.

Scarf Heart
Materials:
Vintage embroidered linen scarf
7" length complementary thread
Sewing machine (optional)

1. Trace pattern onto stitched area of scarf and cut out. Repeat once.
2. Pin with right sides of fabric together, and sew, using a ¼" seam allowance and leaving a 1½" opening for turning. Clip curves and turn right-side out.
3. Stuff with polyester filling and whipstitch opening closed.
4. Thread needle with thread, insert through top center of heart, and tie a knot in thread ends to form hanger.

Muslin Angel
Materials:
6" x 12" piece muslin
2½" x 6" piece fusible interfacing
21" length ⅝"-wide eyelet ruffle trim
26" length ⅛"-wide gold braid
Small amount Spanish moss
11 small cream-colored buttons in assorted shapes and sizes
Thread to match muslin
Tacky glue
Permanent-ink pens, colors: black, red
Sewing machine (optional)

1. Place muslin atop patterns, and lightly trace around patterns on muslin, tracing two of each pattern piece. Cut out muslin pieces. Place right sides of heart pieces together and sew ⅛" from edge, leaving a space for turning where indicated on pattern. Repeat for head and wing pieces, except cut one wing from interfacing and iron interfacing wing to wrong side of one muslin wing before placing wing pieces with right sides together. Clip curves and turn right-side out. Stuff head and heart **only** with polyester filling. (**Note:** Wings will remain unstuffed.) Whipstitch openings closed.

2. Lightly draw eyes, nose, and mouth on face, using black pen for eyes and nose and red pen for mouth.

3. Sew buttons to heart, placing as desired.

4. Glue gold braid around edges of wings and heart. Glue Spanish moss to top one-third of angel's head and along sides of head. Let dry. Cut moss to shape hair, and glue braid around angel's head to form halo. Glue ruffle trim to back side of wings and heart, letting edge of trim extend approximately ½" beyond edges of wings and heart.

5. Sew angel's neck to wings, as indicated on pattern.

6. Apply glue to back side of heart, center heart below head, and press heart in place. Let dry.

7. Insert needle and 7" length of thread through top center of angel's head, and tie a knot in thread ends to form hanger.

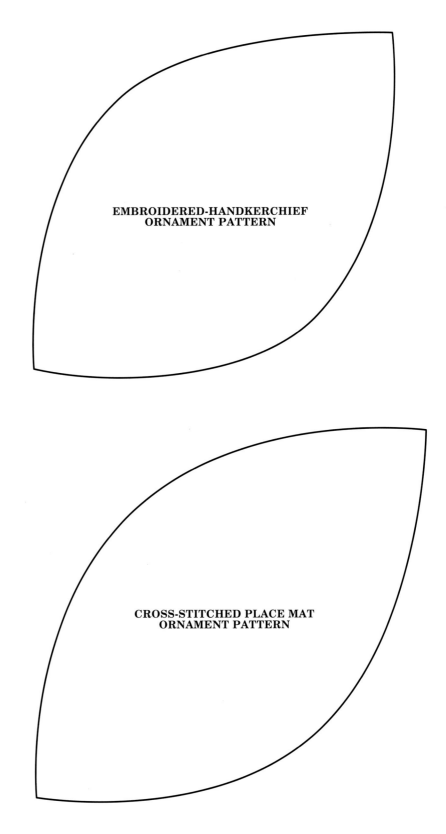

EMBROIDERED-HANDKERCHIEF ORNAMENT PATTERN

CROSS-STITCHED PLACE MAT ORNAMENT PATTERN

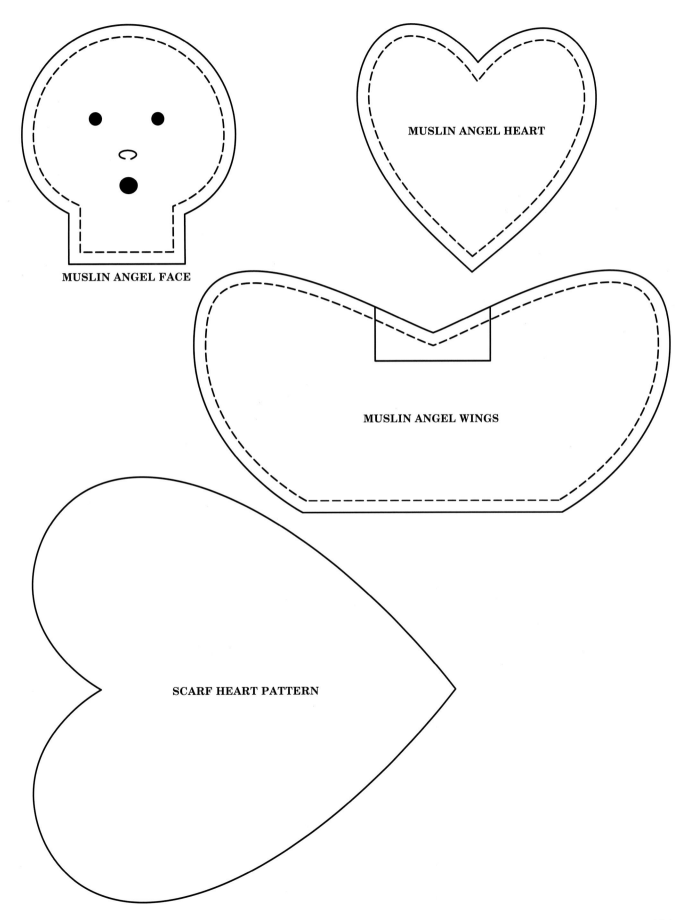

MUSLIN ANGEL FACE

MUSLIN ANGEL HEART

MUSLIN ANGEL WINGS

SCARF HEART PATTERN

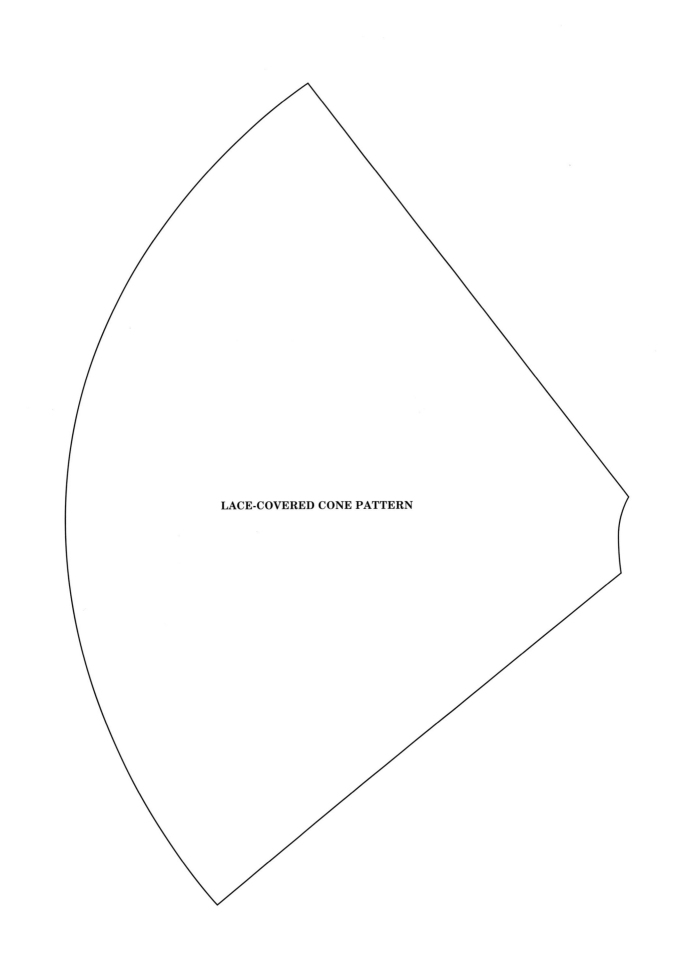

LACE-COVERED CONE PATTERN

Holiday Appliqué

Adorable appliqué designs were used to create the charmers shown on this and the following page. These quick-to-complete ornaments were fashioned using popular motifs and scraps of fabrics in traditional colors. Their flat finishing makes them just right for slipping inside your holiday greetings—what a wonderful way to send Christmas cheer! We've included a circular pattern for those who prefer this shape to a simple square.

Materials:

5"-square fabric scraps in assorted colors of your choice (**Note:** Cut two pieces of same color for **each** ornament.)
Assorted fabric scraps (for appliqué)
Heat 'n Bond™ fusible iron-on adhesive
Quilt batting
Thread and embroidery floss to match fabric scraps
14" length ⅛"-wide red satin ribbon (for **each** ornament)
Hand-sewing needle
Straight pins
Tracing paper
Pencil
Scissors
Sewing machine   Iron

Option: These ornaments can also be made in a circular form. Cut 5½" circles of fabric, and appliqué following instructions. Turn to page **130** for circle pattern.

1. Fuse Heat 'n Bond™ to wrong side of fabric for appliqué.
2. Trace appliqué shapes onto paper side of Heat 'n Bond™. Cut out shapes along tracing lines.
3. Remove paper backing, place shape in center of fabric, and fuse in place.
4. Work buttonhole stitch around shapes, using two strands of embroidery floss in colors to match shapes.

5. Work stem stitch for vein lines in holly leaves and apple, using two strands light-green floss. Work stem stitch on snowman's hat, using two strands matching green floss. Work French knots for snowman's eyes and nose, using two strands black floss. Use four strands black floss for French-knot buttons. Backstitch mouth using two strands black floss. To make scarf, thread six strands green floss in needle. Draw needle down at one side of neck and up on other side. Repeat. Pull ends of floss to one side of neck and tie a knot. Trim ends of floss.
6. Pin quilt batting to wrong side of backing fabric. Place appliquéd front and backing with right sides together. Sew pieces together, using a ⅝" seam allowance and leaving a 1½" opening for turning. Trim seam, clip curves on round pieces, and turn right-side out. Whipstitch opening closed.
7. Cut ribbon 6" long, fold in half, and tack ends to top center of ornament to form hanger. Tie a bow with remaining ribbon and tack to base of ribbon hanger.

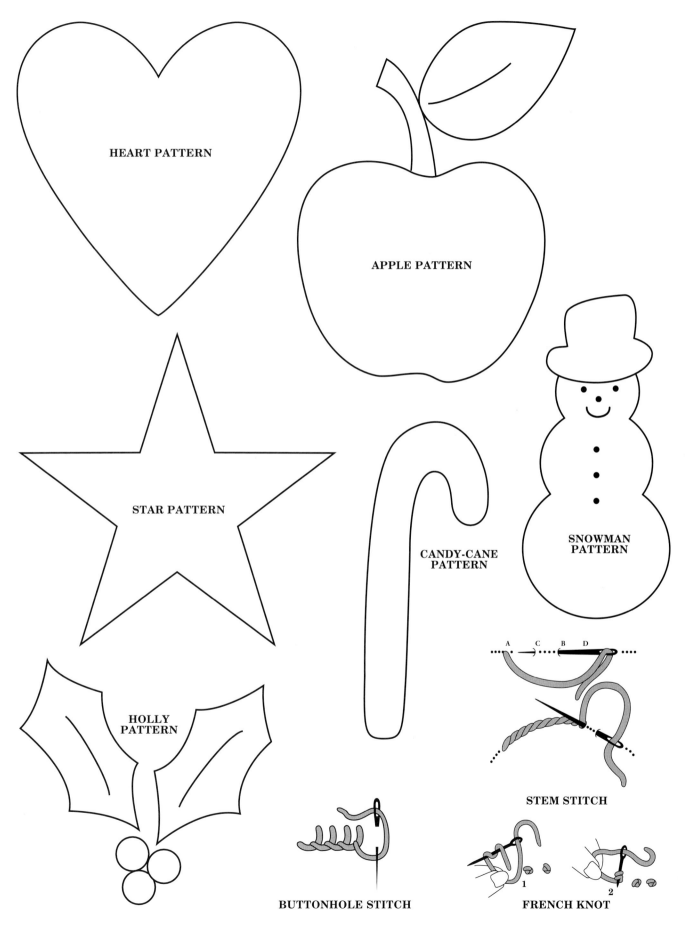

HEART PATTERN

APPLE PATTERN

STAR PATTERN

CANDY-CANE
PATTERN

SNOWMAN
PATTERN

HOLLY
PATTERN

A   C   B D

STEM STITCH

BUTTONHOLE STITCH

1   2

FRENCH KNOT

Stenciled Ornaments

Whether the look you love is positively Christmassy or down-right country, these pleasing ornament designs will delight you! Crafted using easy stencil patterns, these pieces will be perfectly at home hung on your evergreen or used to add a festive touch to an unexpected spot. A smaller, alternate version is also offered, with the stencil pattern placed on point.

Note: For these projects, a general materials list and instructions have been given. Specific materials and instructions for each project have been listed separately.

General materials:
Stencil adhesive
Black permanent-ink pen
Straight pins
Hand-sewing needle
Polyester filling
Thread to match muslin
Scissors
Sharp craft knife
Small stencil brush
Paper towels
Sewing machine   Tacky glue

General Stenciling Instructions:
Blank stencil should be ½"–1" larger on all sides than design to be cut. Center pattern under Mylar® or other blank stencil sheet and trace design using black, permanent-ink pen. Place stencil on hard, smooth cutting area, such as glass or hard board. Use sharp craft knife to cut out areas marked with an *X* on pattern.

When more than one stencil is used, align broken line on second stencil with appropriate portion of first stencil for placement to be correct. Draw second design and cut out.

After stencil is cut, apply stencil adhesive to back of stencil, following directions on adhesive. Center stencil atop item being stenciled and press in place, making sure all cut edges are securely attached.

Dip small stencil brush into paint and wipe excess paint onto paper towel. Brush should be almost dry. Beginning on outside edges of cut-out area, apply paint, using circular motion. If darker color is needed, dip brush in paint again, wipe off excess, and continue brushing until shade desired is acquired. Remove stencil. Let paint dry. If using second stencil, let paint dry on first area before continuing. Secure second stencil, being careful to align with markings of first stencil, and paint in same manner. Let dry.

Pineapple
Materials:
Two 5" squares muslin
Two 5" squares Mylar®

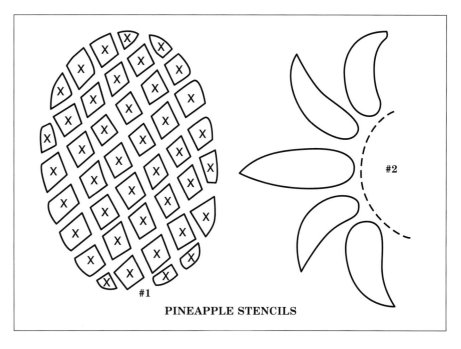

PINEAPPLE STENCILS

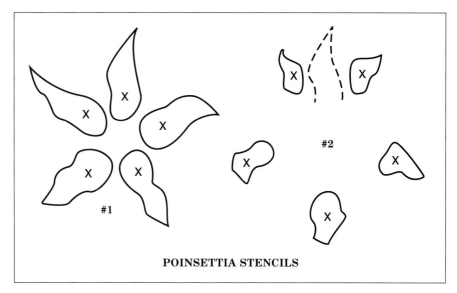

POINSETTIA STENCILS

Acrylic paint, colors: green, yellow, brown
18" length ⅛" metallic-gold cord
7" length gold thread

1. Prepare stencils referring to General Stenciling Instructions. Place stencil #1 on one muslin square and paint yellow. Lightly paint brown over some of the yellow areas. Place stencil #2 and paint green.
2. Place ornament front and back with right sides of muslin together. Sew around edges, using a ⅝" seam allowance and leaving a 1½" opening for turning. Trim corners and turn right-side out. Stuff lightly with polyester filling and whipstitch opening closed.
3. Glue gold cord along seam line.
4. Thread needle with gold thread, insert through top center, and tie a knot in thread ends to form hanger.

Poinsettia
Materials:
Two 5" squares muslin
Two 4" squares Mylar®
Acrylic paint, colors: green, red
Four 3mm yellow pom-poms
24" length ⅛"-wide gold cord
7" length gold thread

TREE STENCIL

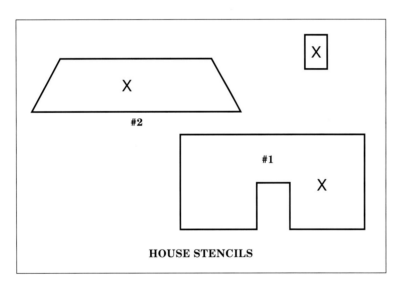

#2

#1

HOUSE STENCILS

1. Prepare stencils referring to General Stenciling Instructions. Place stencil #1 on muslin and paint red. Place stencil #2 and paint green.
2. Place ornament front and back with right sides of muslin together. Sew around edges, using a ⅝" seam allowance and leaving a 1½" opening for turning. Trim corners and turn right-side out. Stuff lightly with polyester filling and whipstitch opening closed.
3. Glue cord along seam line. Make bow from remainder of cord and tack near top center of ornament. Glue pom-poms in center of poinsettia.
4. Thread needle with gold thread, insert through top center, and tie a knot in thread ends to form hanger.

Tree
Materials:
Two 5" squares muslin
5" square Mylar®
Acrylic paint, color: green
Fifteen 3mm red pom-poms
16" length red knitting yarn

1. Prepare stencil referring to General Stenciling Instructions. Center stencil atop muslin and paint green.
2. Place ornament front and back with right sides of muslin together. Sew around edges, using a ⅝" seam allowance and leaving a 1½" opening for turning. Trim corners and turn right-side out. Stuff lightly with polyester filling and whipstitch opening closed.
3. Glue yarn along seam line. Glue pom-poms on tree, referring to photo on page **126** for placement.
4. Thread needle with 7"-length thread, insert through top center, and tie a knot in thread ends to form hanger.

House
Materials:
Two 5" squares muslin
Two 4" squares Mylar®
Acrylic paint, colors: dark blue, red
8" length ¼"-wide blue ribbon
Blue embroidery floss

1. Prepare stencils referring to General Stenciling Instructions. Place stencil #1 on muslin and paint blue. Place stencil #2 and paint red.
2. Place ornament front and back with right sides of muslin together.

Sew around edges, using a ⅝" seam allowance and leaving a 1½" opening for turning. Trim corners and turn right-side out. Stuff lightly with polyester filling and whipstitch opening closed.

3. Work buttonhole stitch around edges of ornament, using three strands blue floss.

4. Make bow with blue ribbon and attach to center top of ornament.

5. Thread needle with 7"-length thread, insert through top center, and tie a knot in thread ends to form hanger.

Bird
Materials:
Two 5" squares muslin
Two 4" squares Mylar®
2" square Mylar®
Acrylic paint, colors: dark yellow, light blue, dark blue
16" length ¼"-wide silver braid
7" length silver thread

1. Prepare stencils referring to General Stenciling Instructions. Place stencil #1 on muslin and paint lightly with dark blue. Place stencil #2 and paint light blue. Place stencil #3 and paint dark yellow.

2. Place ornament front and back with right sides of muslin together. Sew around edges, using a ⅝" seam allowance and leaving a 1½" opening for turning. Trim corners and turn right-side out. Stuff lightly with polyester filling and whipstitch opening closed.

3. Glue braid along seam line.

4. Thread needle with silver thread, insert through top center, and tie a knot in thread ends to form hanger.

Bell
Materials:
Two 4" squares muslin
Two 3" squares Mylar®
Acrylic paint, colors: red, metallic gold
8" length ⅛"-wide metallic ribbon
Metallic-gold sewing-machine thread

Option: The bell was made with the stencil placed diagonally. It can be made to match the remaining ornaments by placing stencils straight and using 5" squares of muslin.

1. Prepare stencils referring to General Stenciling Instructions. Place stencil #1 on muslin and paint red.

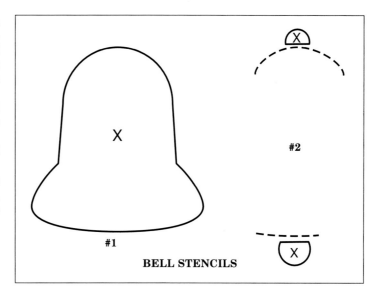

BELL STENCILS

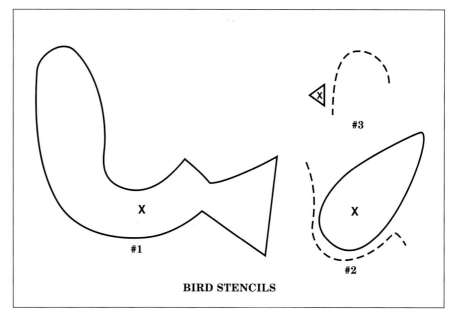

BIRD STENCILS

Place stencil #2 and paint metallic gold.

2. Place ornament front and back with right sides of muslin together. Sew around edges, using a ⅝" seam allowance and leaving a 1½" opening for turning. Trim corners and turn right-side out. Stuff lightly with polyester filling and whipstitch opening closed.

3. Thread needle with off-white thread and stitch around design.

4. Work buttonhole stitch around edges of ornament, using two strands metallic-gold thread.

5. Make bow with metallic ribbon and tack at top of bell. Trim ends.

6. Thread needle with metallic-gold thread, insert through top center, and tie a knot in thread ends to form hanger.

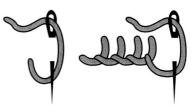

BUTTONHOLE STITCH

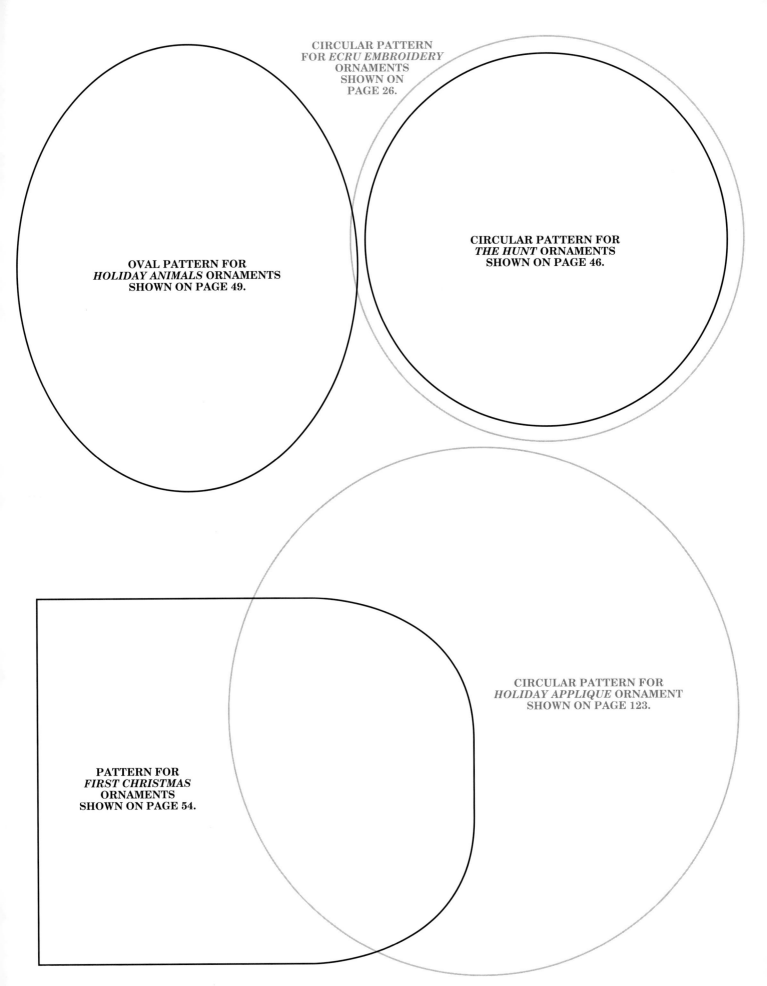

CIRCULAR PATTERN
FOR *ECRU EMBROIDERY*
ORNAMENTS
SHOWN ON
PAGE 26.

OVAL PATTERN FOR
HOLIDAY ANIMALS **ORNAMENTS**
SHOWN ON PAGE 49.

CIRCULAR PATTERN FOR
THE HUNT **ORNAMENTS**
SHOWN ON PAGE 46.

CIRCULAR PATTERN FOR
HOLIDAY APPLIQUE ORNAMENT
SHOWN ON PAGE 123.

PATTERN FOR
FIRST CHRISTMAS
ORNAMENTS
SHOWN ON PAGE 54.

Basic Ornament-
Finishing Instructions

General materials:
Polyester filling
Thread to match fabric and trim
Hand-sewing needle
Scissors
Sewing machine
Iron

Note: Please read all instructions carefully before beginning. Use a ¼" seam allowance throughout unless otherwise noted.

1. Press ornament from back.

2. For those ornaments that require a pattern, center ornament pattern atop stitched design and lightly mark around edge of pattern. Remove pattern and make second marking ¼" inside first. First marking is cutting line. Second marking is stitching line.

For those ornaments whose shapes will follow the perimeter of the stitched design, determine how far out from the edge of stitched design you wish edge of ornament to be. Mark distance slightly outside measurement and evenly around entire design, using tailor's chalk or disappearing-ink fabric-marking pen and marking carefully along straight grain of fabric.

3. Place ornament front right-side up atop facing fabric. **Note:** If a design is stitched on linen or evenweave, you may need to add a facing before design is finished as an ornament. Ornaments stitched on Aida are often stiff enough to omit facing. Either a sew-in, non-woven interfacing or a solid-color cotton fabric with some stiffness makes a good facing for the more "open" cross-stitch fabrics. Fusible interfacing is not suitable.

Pin stitched front to facing fabric, making sure fabric is straight and smooth. Use needle and one strand of thread to hand sew facing fabric to ornament along marked line. (**Note:** Sewing by hand will hold ornament straight. Machine sewing at this point can distort the piece.) Remove pins.

4. To finish ornament without piping, lace, etc., in the seam, place ornament atop backing fabric, placing right sides of fabric together. Pin. (**Note:** Backing fabric should be slightly larger all around than assembled stitched design and facing plus seam allowance.) **Do not** cut out ornament. Machine- or hand-sew just inside hand-sewn line, leaving an opening at top for turning. Remove pins. Turn right-side out. (**Note:** If shape of ornament is square or rectangular, trim fabric diagonally across corners close to stitching before turning right-side out.) Press carefully along edges and then entire surface, using a press cloth to cover ornament. Stuff ornament with polyester filling, if desired.

Cut a 7" length of floss, bring floss ends together to form hanger, and tie a knot in floss ends. Whipstitch opening in top of ornament closed, taking small, neat stitches, turning raw edges of fabric under evenly to inside of ornament, and securing hanger at top, center of ornament.

5. To finish ornament with piping or other trim around outside edge, determine distance desired between edge of stitched design and side seam. Measure

piping or other trim between its stitching line and raw edge. Add this measurement to the first one and mark this distance out from edge of stitched design. Lay piping or other trim with its raw edge along marked line and its finished edge toward center of ornament.

Beginning approximately ¾" from cut end, sew piping or other trim to stitched front, sewing along existing stitching line. Use an iron, if necessary, to steam piping or other trim into shape. Shape corners carefully as you sew, leaving enough piping or other trim at corners to turn ornament right-side out. When you have sewn to within ¾" of first end of piping or other trim, overlap 1" and cut off. Remove stitches in piping to open one end of piping and expose cord within. Hold cord to the point where it would cross the other cord and cut off. Butt ends of cord together and fold loose piping fabric over both, turning raw edge of fabric under. For other trims, overlap neatly, turning raw edges under.

Continue to sew around ornament. Cut backing fabric as in #4. Sew assembled front and backing fabric together, using hand-sewn line as a guide for stitching and placing right sides of fabric together. If using a sewing machine, using a zipper foot will enable you to sew closer to cord than if using a regular foot. Complete ornament as in #4.

Note: This method can be used for adding lace, rick-rack, ruffles, or any other embellishment that is sewn into a seam.

General Instructions for Crochet

Crochet Abbreviations:

beg—begin(ning)
bet—between
ch—chain stitch
ch- —refers to chain previously
   made
cont—continue
dc—double crochet
est—established
hdc—half double crochet
lp(s)—loop(s)
nxt—next
rep(s)—repeat(s)
rnd(s)—round(s)
sc—single crochet
sk—skip
sl st—slip stitch
sp(s)—space(s)
st(s)—stitch(es)
tog—together
tr—treble or triple crochet
WS—wrong side(s)
yo—yarn over

Repeat whatever follows * as indicated. "Rep from * 3 times more" means to work 4 times in all. Work directions given in parentheses and brackets the number of times specified or in the place specified.

Gauge

Before beginning a project, work a gauge swatch using the recommended-size hook. Count and compare the number of stitches per inch in the swatch with the designer's gauge. If you have fewer stitches in your swatch, try a smaller hook; if you have more stitches, try a larger hook.

Working Together

Hold the hook as you would a pencil or a piece of chalk. Weave the yarn through the fingers of your left hand to control the amount of yarn fed into the work and to provide tension. Once work has begun, the thumb and middle finger of the left hand come into play, pressing together to hold the stitches just made.

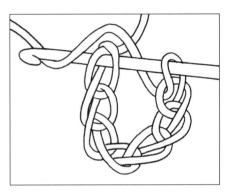

Slip-Stitch Illustration

Here a slip stitch (sl st) is used to join a ring. Taking care not to twist ch, insert hook into first ch, yo and pull through ch and lp on hook (sl st made). The sl st can also be used to join finished pieces or to move across a group of sts without adding height to the work.

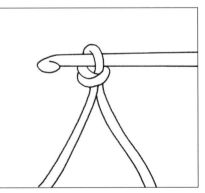

Slip-Knot Illustrations

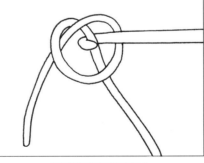

ILLUSTRATION A

ILLUSTRATION B

Loop the yarn around and let the loose end of the yarn fall behind the loop to form a pretzel shape, as shown. Insert the hook (Illustration A) and pull both ends to close the knot (Illustration B).

Chain-Stitch Illustrations

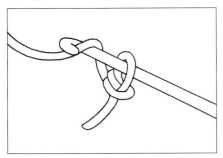

ILLUSTRATION A

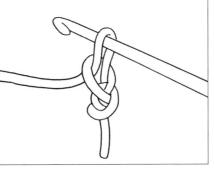

ILLUSTRATION B

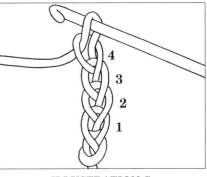

ILLUSTRATION C

A. Place a slip knot on your hook. With hands in the position shown in Working Together, and with the thumb and middle finger of the left hand holding the yarn end, wrap the yarn up and over the hook (from back to front). This movement is called a "yarn over (yo)" and is basic to every crochet stitch.

B. Use the hook to pull the yarn through the loop (lp) already on the hook. The combination of yo and pulling the yarn through the lp makes one chain stitch (ch).

C. Repeat until the chain is the desired length, trying to keep the movements even and relaxed, and all the ch stitches (sts) the same size. Hold the ch near the working area to keep it from twisting. Count sts as shown in illustration. (Do not count lp on hook or slip knot.)

Single-Crochet Illustrations

ILLUSTRATION A

ILLUSTRATION B

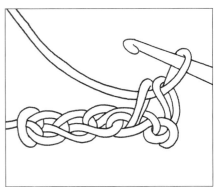

ILLUSTRATION C

A. Insert hook under top 2 lps of 2nd ch from hook and yo. (Always work sts through top 2 lps unless directions specify otherwise.)

B. Pull yarn through ch (2 lps on hook).

C. Yo and pull yarn through 2 lps on hook (1 sc made).

Half-Double-Crochet Illustrations

ILLUSTRATION A

ILLUSTRATION B

ILLUSTRATION C

A. Yo and insert hook into 3rd ch from hook.

B. Yo and pull through ch (3 lps on hook).

C. Yo and pull yarn through all 3 lps on hook (1 hdc made).

Double-Crochet Illustrations

ILLUSTRATION A

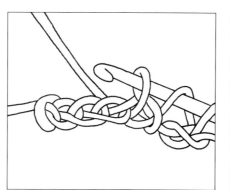

ILLUSTRATION B

ILLUSTRATION C

A. Yo, insert hook into 4th ch from hook, and yo.

B. Pull yarn through ch (3 lps on hook).

C. Yo and pull through 2 lps on hook (2 lps remaining).
Note: When directions say "keeping last lp of each st on hook," this means to work the specified st to the final yo. This is done to make a cluster or to work a decrease.

ILLUSTRATION D

D. Yo and pull through 2 remaining (rem) lps (1 dc made).

Triple-Crochet Diagrams

A. Yo twice, insert hook into 5th ch from hook. Yo and pull through ch (4 lps on hook).

B. Yo and pull through 2 lps on hook (3 lps rem). Yo and pull through 2 lps on hook (2 lps rem). Yo and pull through 2 lps on hook (1 tr made).

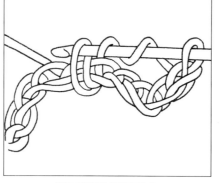

ILLUSTRATION A

ILLUSTRATION B

General Instructions for Knitting

Knitting Abbreviations and Terms:

bo—bind off
co—cast on
inc—increase
k—knit
nxt—next
p—purl
rem—remain(ing)
RS—right side
sl—slip
st(s)—stitch(es)
tog—together
WS—wrong side
yo—yarn over

Casting On
Slip Knot

ILLUSTRATION A

A. Pull a 10" length of yarn from the skein. Lay the end of the yarn on a table and make a circle over it.

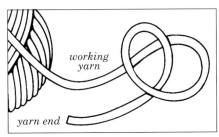

ILLUSTRATION B

B. Place the working yarn under the circle.

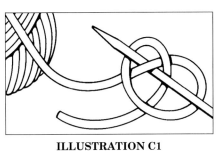

ILLUSTRATION C1

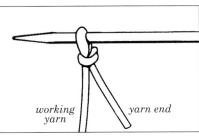

ILLUSTRATION C2

C. Put a needle under the bar just made (Illustration C1), and pull on both ends of the yarn to complete the slip knot (Illustration C2).

Holding Yarn

Two methods of knitting are included—holding the working yarn in the right hand (English Method, Illustration A) or in the left hand (Continental Method, Illustration B). Try both methods to determine which feels more comfortable. The English Method uses the right hand more and requires less dexterity of the left hand. The Continental Method requires some dexterity of the left hand and is believed by some to be faster. Either method will be slightly awkward at first, but with practice will become easier and your work will be more even.

English Method

Continental Method

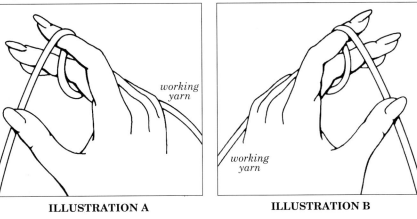

ILLUSTRATION A

ILLUSTRATION B

Casting On (continued)

English Method

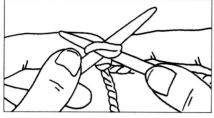

ILLUSTRATION A

A. Hold the needle with the slip knot in your left hand. Hold the empty needle and the working yarn in your right hand. Insert the right needle into the front of the slip knot from left to right.

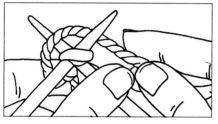

ILLUSTRATION B

B. Hold the right needle with your left thumb and index finger. With your right hand, bring the working yarn beneath the right needle and between needles from back to front.

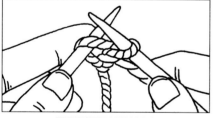

ILLUSTRATION C

C. With your right hand, bring the right needle, with the loop of yarn, toward you and through the stitch.

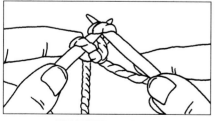

ILLUSTRATION D

D. Bring the left needle forward and up into the new loop from bottom to top, allowing the right needle to slide out.

Continental Method

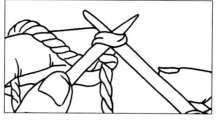

ILLUSTRATION A

A. Hold the working yarn and the needle with the slip knot in your left hand. Hold the empty needle in your right hand. Insert the right needle into the front of the slip knot from left to right.

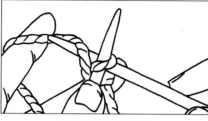

ILLUSTRATION B

B. With your index finger, bring the working yarn between the needles from left to right.

ILLUSTRATION C

C. Bring the right needle, with the loop of yarn, toward you and through the stitch.

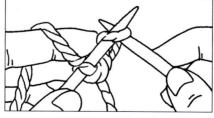

ILLUSTRATION D

D. Bring the left needle forward and up into the new loop from bottom to top, allowing the right needle to slide out.

Both Methods

It is important to slide the stitch over the tapered tip to the long needle shaft, then pull the yarn slightly (so there are no loose loops of yarn), but not too tightly because you want your cast-on row to be as elastic as your knitting.

Knitting

English Method

A. Hold the needle with the cast-on stitches in your left hand and the empty needle in your right hand.
B. With the yarn in back of the needles, insert the right needle into the front of the stitch closest to the tip of the left needle from left to right, just as you did when you were casting on.
C. Hold the right needle with your left thumb and index finger while you bring the yarn beneath the right needle and between the needles from back to front.
D. With your right hand, bring the right needle, with the loop of yarn, toward you and through the stitch.
E. You now have a new stitch on the right needle, so slip the old stitch off the left needle (Illustration E).
F. Tighten the new stitch on the shaft of the right needle.

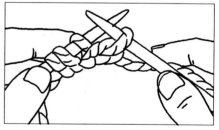

ILLUSTRATION E

Continental Method
A. Hold the needle with the cast-on stitches in your left hand and the empty needle in your right hand.
B. With the yarn in back of the needles, insert the right needle into the front of the stitch closest to the tip of the left needle from left to right, just as you did when you were casting on.

C. With your index finger, bring the yarn between the needles from left to right.

D. Bring the right needle, with the loop of yarn, toward you and through the stitch.

E. You now have a new stitch on the right needle, so slip the old stitch off the left needle (Illustration E).

F. Tighten the new stitch on the shaft of the right needle.

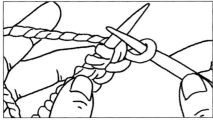

ILLUSTRATION E

Both Methods

Repeat Steps B–F across the row. You should have 10 stitches; count them to make sure you did not pick up any extra loops along the way.

To begin the next row, hold the empty needle in your right hand and the needle with the stitches in your left hand. The working yarn hangs straight down from the stitch closest to the tip of the needle (Illustration F). Repeat Steps B–F across the row.

After knitting a few more rows, look closely at your knitting. You will see that each stitch looks like the outlined stitch in Illustration G.

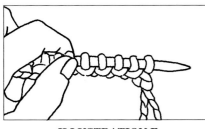

ILLUSTRATION F

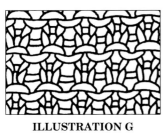

ILLUSTRATION G

Purling

English Method

A. Hold the needle with the stitches in your left hand and the empty needle in your right hand.

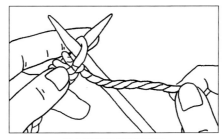

ILLUSTRATION B

B. With the yarn in front of the needles, insert the right needle into the front of the stitch from right to left.

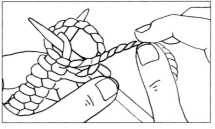

ILLUSTRATION C

C. Hold the right needle with your left thumb and index finger while you bring the yarn between the needles from right to left and around the right needle.

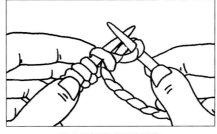

ILLUSTRATION D

D. Move the right needle, with the loop of yarn, through the stitch and away from you, slipping the old stitch off the left needle. Tighten this new stitch on the shaft of the right needle.

Continental Method

A. Hold the needle with the stitches in your left hand and the empty needle in your right hand.

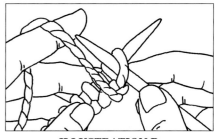

ILLUSTRATION B

B. With the yarn in front of the needles, insert the right needle into the front of the stitch from right to left.

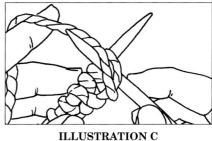

ILLUSTRATION C

C. With your index finger, bring the yarn between the needles from right to left and around the right needle.

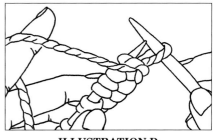

ILLUSTRATION D

D. Move the right needle, with the loop of yarn, through the stitch and away from you, slipping the old stitch off the left needle. Tighten this new stitch on the shaft of the right needle.

Both Methods

Repeat Steps B–D across the row.

Binding Off

All knitting ends with binding off; locking each stitch as you remove it from the needle. Binding off is also used to work buttonholes and pockets and for shaping.

A. Knit 2 stitches.

B. With the left needle, bring the first stitch over the second stitch and off the needle (Illustrations B1 and B2).

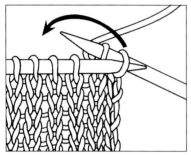

ILLUSTRATION B1

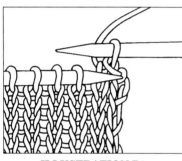

ILLUSTRATION B2

C. Knit the next stitch. Repeat Steps B and C until only one stitch remains on the right needle.

D. To lock the last stitch, cut the yarn (leaving a long end) and bring it through the stitch, pulling to tighten.

It's very important for the bind off to be as elastic as your knitting.

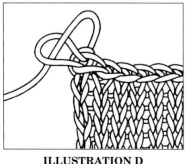

ILLUSTRATION D

Slip Stitch

When the instructions state slip a stitch, you simply transfer it from one needle to another—generally, from the left needle to the right needle, without knitting or purling it.

Increasing
Knit Increases
1. Bar Increase

Knit the next stitch but do not slip it off the left needle (Illustration 1A). Instead, knit into the back of the same stitch (Illustration 1B) and slip it off the left needle.

The Bar Increase is the most popular and, perhaps, the easiest of increases. It is often used at the beginning and at the end of a row where it probably would be hidden in a seam.

ILLUSTRATION 1A

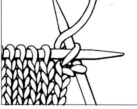

ILLUSTRATION 1B

BAR INCREASE

YARN-OVER INCREASE

2. Yarn Over-Increase (abbreviated yo)

A yarn over is simply placing the yarn over the right needle, creating an extra stitch.

On the row following a yarn over, you must be careful to keep it on the needle and treat it as a stitch by knitting or purling it as instructed.

Purl Increases
1. Bar Increase

Purl the next stitch but do not slip it off the left needle. Insert the right needle into the back loop of the same stitch from back to front and purl it. Slip it off the needle.

ILLUSTRATION 1

2. Invisible Increases
Right Invisible Increase

Insert the right needle from the back into the top of the stitch below the next stitch on the left needle (Illustration 2A) and purl it.

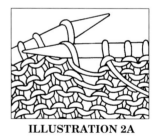

ILLUSTRATION 2A

Left Invisible Increase

Insert the left needle from the front into the top of the stitch 2 rows below the stitch on the right needle (Illustration 2B), pull it up and purl it.

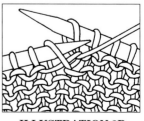

ILLUSTRATION 2B

Yarn Overs

1. When a yo falls between 2 knit stitches, work as follows:

Bring the yarn forward between the needles, then back over the top of the right needle, so that it is now in position to knit the next stitch.

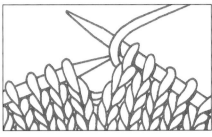

ILLUSTRATION 1

2. When a yo falls after a knit stitch and before a purl stitch, work as follows:

Bring the yarn forward between the needles, then back over the top of the right needle and forward between the needles again, so that it is in position to purl the next stitch.

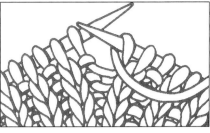

ILLUSTRATION 2

3. When a yo falls between 2 purl stitches, work as follows:

Take the yarn over the right needle to the back, then forward under it, so that it is now in position to purl the next stitch.

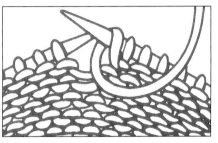

ILLUSTRATION 3

4. When a yo falls after a purl stitch and before a knit stitch, work as follows:

Take the yarn over the right needle to the back, so that it is now in position to knit the next stitch.

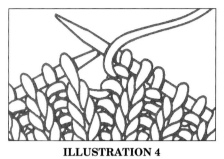

ILLUSTRATION 4

Weaving in Yarn Ends

Turn your project wrong-side out. Thread a yarn needle with the yarn end and weave it through several stitches in the seam. If desired, reverse directions and weave it back through 2 or 3 more stitches. Clip the yarn close to the work.

Basic Stitch Diagrams

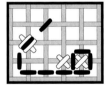

Backstitch (across two ¾ stitches and around full cross)

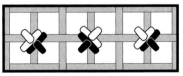

Two ¾ Stitches (in one square, using two different floss colors)

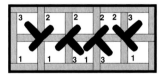

¾ Cross Stitches (over one in various positions)

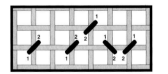

¼ Cross Stitch (over two threads)

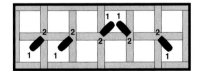

¼ Cross Stitch (over one thread)

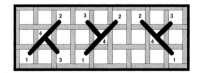

¾ Cross Stitch (over two threads)

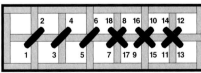

Full Cross Stitch (over one thread)

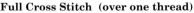

Full Cross Stitch (over two threads)

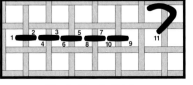

Basic Backstitch

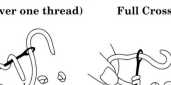

French Knot

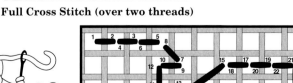

Backstitch (showing variations)

General Instructions for Cross Stitch

Basic Supplies: Even-weave fabric, tapestry needle(s), six-strand embroidery floss, embroidery scissors, embroidery hoop (optional).

Fabric Preparation: The instructions and yardage for finishing materials have been written and calculated for each of the projects shown stitched on the fabric listed in each color code. Alternate fabric choices have also been listed. If you wish to stitch a design on an alternate fabric, or alter its placement, you will need to recalculate the finished size of the project, as well as the yardage of finishing materials needed, and make the necessary dimension adjustments when finishing.

Determine size of fabric needed for a project by dividing number of horizontal stitches by thread count of fabric. For example, if a design 35 stitches wide is worked on 14-count fabric, it will cover 2½" (35 divided by 14 equals 2½). Repeat process for vertical count. Add three inches on all sides of design area to find dimensions for cutting fabric. Whipstitch edges to prevent fraying.

Floss Preparation: Cut floss into 14" to 18" lengths. Separate all six strands. Reunite number of strands needed and thread needle, leaving one floss end longer than the other.

Where to Start: Start wherever you like! Some designers suggest finding center of fabric and starting there. Others recommend beginning with a central motif, while still others work borders first. Many find fabric center, count up

and back to the left, and start with the uppermost left stitch. Wherever you begin, be sure to leave allowance for all horizontal and vertical stitches so that a 3" fabric margin is left around completed design.

Should you choose to begin at the center point, find it by folding fabric from top to bottom and then from left to right. Use a straight pin to mark upper-left corner at junction of folds, and then unfold fabric. Pin will be in center of fabric.

After deciding where to begin on fabric, find same point on graph. Each square on graph represents one stitch. Those squares containing a symbol (i.e., X,T,O) indicate that a stitch should be made in that space over those threads. Different symbols represent different colors of floss for stitches. (See color code of chart.) They may also indicate partial or decorative stitches. Familiarize yourself with color code before you begin stitching. Even-weave fabric may be stretched over an embroidery hoop to facilitate stitching.

Stitching the Design: Using the diagrams on page **139,** stitch design, completing all full and partial cross stitches first. Cross all full cross stitches in same direction to achieve a smooth surface appearance. Work backstitches second, and any decorative stitches last.

Helpful Hints for Stitching: Do not knot floss. Instead, catch end on back of work with first few stitches. As you stitch, pull floss through fabric "holes" with one stroke, not several short ones. The moment you

feel resistance from floss, cease pulling. Consistent tension on floss results in a smoother look for stitches. Drop your needle frequently to allow floss to untwist. It twists naturally as you stitch and, as it gets shorter, must be allowed to untwist more often. To begin a new color on project, prepare floss and secure new strands as noted. To end stitching, run floss under several completed stitches and clip remaining strands close to surface. Many times it is necessary to skip a few spaces (threads) on the fabric in order to continue a row of stitches in the same color. If you must skip an area covering more than ¼", end stitching as described and begin again at next point. This procedure prevents uneven tension on the embroidery surface and snagging on the back. It also keeps colors from showing through unstitched areas. Do not carry thread over an area that will remain unstitched.

When You Are Finished: For designs using cotton or linen floss on cotton or linen even-weave fabric, hand wash piece with mild detergent in warm water. Rinse thoroughly with cold water. Roll in terry towel and squeeze gently to remove excess moisture. Do not wring. Unroll towel and allow piece to dry until barely damp. Iron on padded surface with design face down, using medium setting for heat. A press cloth will help prevent shine on dark fabrics. **Note:** Acrylics, acrylic blends, wools, or silks must be treated differently when cleaning. Check manufacturer's guidelines for special cleaning instructions.

How-Tos for Making Twisted Cording

To make cording trim for ornaments, you will need one skein of floss in the color of your choice for each ornament you wish to trim. (**Note:** Multiple floss colors and assorted fibers can be combined if desired.) When selecting floss colors, refer to color codes to achieve exact color matches.

Begin by unwinding entire skein of floss. Bring the two raw ends together, dividing floss length in half, so that you have two main threads consisting of six strands each. Fold in half again, and then once more, smoothing each time as if folding a blanket. At this point, one end of floss will have raw edges, the other loops (Illustration 1). Tie a knot in the end with raw edges and loop over top of chair (Illustration 2). To twist, insert fingers through center of looped end and move wrist in a circular motion (Illustration 3). Continue twisting until floss tightens around fingers. Remove fingers until just one remains in floss. Remove floss from finger without letting go of twist in floss. Hand twist the remaining portion. Bring the two ends together again, holding securely and dividing in the middle with one finger (Illustration 4). Remove end with raw edges from back of chair. Remove finger from middle dividing point. Floss will twist. When it stops twisting, run hand over length of floss several times to smooth, and tie a knot in raw-edge end to hold twist (Illustration 5). Whipstitch to perimeter of ornaments, making a hanging loop at top of ornament or leaving a twisted-floss tail to attach an ornament hanger.

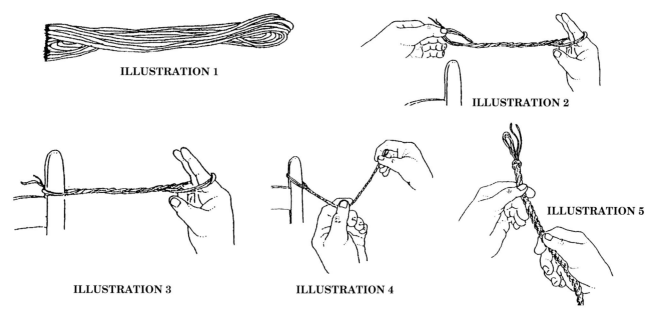

ILLUSTRATION 1

ILLUSTRATION 2

ILLUSTRATION 3

ILLUSTRATION 4

ILLUSTRATION 5

Acknowledgements

Grateful acknowledgement of their generosity is extended to the following companies and individuals, who have provided materials for the production of the models and the props and locations used for photographing them.

AK Designs
Attic Antiques
Bobby D.'s Christmas Trees
Bridge's Antiques

The Caron Collection
Coats & Clark
Craft World® International, Inc.
Danny and Rita Stone
The DMC Corporation
Euroflax, Inc.
FibreCraft
Gatehouse Gift Shop
Gay Bowles Sales
The Holly Tree
JBC Tree Farm
Keith and Allison Kearney

Kreinik Manufacturing Company, Inc.
Loose Ends
Massey's Corral
Needle Necessities
Paul and Pat McKleroy
Primitive Artisan
Rich's
Robert Rothschild Berry Farm, Inc.
Wichelt Imports, Inc.
Yarn Tree Designs
YLI Corporation
Zweigart®

Shopper's Guide

Items not included in "Shopper's Guide" are either commonly available, antiques, or from private collections. Antiques included in "Shopper's Guide" were available from the merchants listed at the time photography was completed. Availability may vary depending on each merchant's sales since that time.

Credits—Designers

Shades of White

Kathie Ballard
Tatted Snowflakes, page 17.

Katherine Eng
A Flurry of Snowflakes, page 30.

Helen Haywood
Petite Guardian Angels, page 24.

Nancy Hearne
Crochet Ornament Covers,
    page 21.

Kathy Holicky for Kreinik
Manufacturing Company, Inc.
Christmas Snowflakes, page 12.

Judi Kauffman
Opals in the Snow, page 18.

Angela Pullen
Ecru Embroidery, page 26.

Jane Viking Swanson
Battenberg Lace Ornaments,
    page 8.

An English Country Christmas

Marie Barber
Holiday Animals, page 49.
The Hunt, page 46.

Angela Pullen
*Needlepoint Angel, Bell, Horse,
    and Sleigh,* page 36.

Hélène Rush
Knitted Christmas Ornaments,
    page 43.

Virginia Soskin
*Needlepoint Violin, Horn, and
    Drum,* page 40.

Holiday Traditions

Marie Barber
First Christmas, page 54.

Charlotte Holder
The First Christmas, page 64.
Nutcracker Beadwork, page 68.
Smocked Flowers & Trees, page 72.

KD Artistry
Holiday Trio, page 75.

Angela Pullen
Candy-Cane Christmas, page 60.

A Very Victorian Yule

Marie Barber
Feathered Friends, page 84.

Ashley C. Cobb
Button Tassels, page 102.

Ann Hallay
*Counterchange Smocked Orna-
    ments,* page 104.

Charlotte Holder
Victorian Silk-Ribbon Treasures,
    page 80.

Angela Pullen
Silk-Ribbon Ball Ornaments,
    page 92.

Linda J. Stirratt
Basic Tassels, page 101.

Anna-Marie Winter for Kreinik
Manufacturing Company, Inc.
Crown-Knot Tassels, page 102.

Claudia B. Wood
Crazy-Quilt Ornaments, page 88.
Gold-Accented Ornaments,
    page 98.
Traditional Nine-Patch Ornaments,
    page 98.

Season's Craftings

Inez Norton
Attic Crafts, page 118.
Holiday Appliqué, page 123.
Quick & Easy Bazaar Ornaments,
    page 115.
Stenciled Ornaments, page 126.
Twelve Days of Christmas,
    page 108.

Credits—Stitchers, Charters, and Seamstresses

Stitching
Jennifer Beaulieu
René Brune
Stephanie Burrows
Cheryl Forman
Denise Hogan
Jill Hooper
Debbie Kendrick
Linda Langston
Vicki McCallen

Lori McGuire
Carol Norris
Patty Owens
Catherine Scott
Linda J. Stirratt
Jean Strickland
April Taylor
Margaret Taylor
Pam Tilton
Linda Weaver

Computer Charting
Debbie Begley
Lea Burks
Rebecca Mitchell
Susan Veerling
Laurie Zeanah

Custom Finishing
Heidi Howlett
Claudia B. Wood

Index

Numbers in **bold** type indicate color-photo pages.
All other numbers refer to pages for charts, color codes, patterns, and instructions.